Side Dishes to be a taste treat
for entrées you can buy.

Choose from Appetizers, Vegetables,
Soups, Salads, Salsas, Chutneys,
and so much more

All it takes is one
side dish
to transform
an entrée into a great meal.

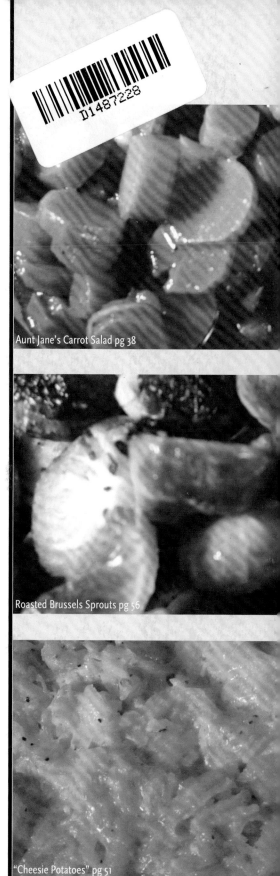

Aunt Jane's Carrot Salad pg 38

Roasted Brussels Sprouts pg 56

"Cheesie Potatoes" pg 51

Pumpkin Soup pg 28

©Connie Hope

Printing © in 2010

ISBN # 13   9780615354132

Printing in China by HX Printing
Jacob D. Hope at jacobhope@hxbookprinting.com

This book was created by Connie Hope
Jacket design by Ed Lain, www.LazerGrafixDesign.com.
Production: Andrea Merkert, amADVERTISINGdesign.com
Illustrations by John W. H. Hope
Photographs by Connie Hope
Edited by Martha Jeffers, The Grammar Granny
Proofread by Hewitt B. McCloskey, Jr.

www.CookingByConnie.com
inadditiontotheentree.blogspot.com

You Can Change a Ho-Hum Meal Into A Great Meal

with your personal favorites from this cookbook.

Here is a key to determine the ease of a recipe for the people who hate to cook and want something easy, or those who need more of a challenge.

    'Hate to cook' Very Easy

    A little more difficult

    The Chef Extraordinaire—difficult

©Connie Hope

©Connie Hope

Table of Contents

©Connie Hope

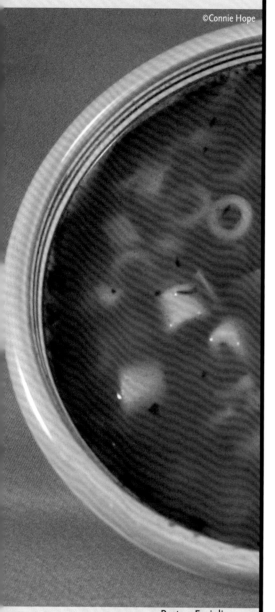
©Connie Hope

Pasta e Fagioli pg 33

©Connie Hope

Artichoke Risotto Pg 53

X. Relishes and Pickles 85

XI Desserts and Breads 97

©Connie Hope

Cucumber Relish pg 94

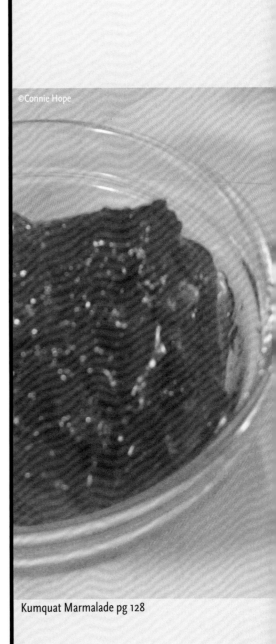

©Connie Hope

Kumquat Marmalade pg 128

©Connie Hope

Basil Pesto pg 128

Acknowledgment:

This book has taken twenty years to write and four years to compile. I want to thank so many people for their support. First, my three children: John, who has done some of the illustrations; Jacob, who has always said I am the greatest cook and "Mom, you should write a recipe book" and Jennifer, who has read and re-read most of the book for 'flow.' I really need to thank my life partner, Hewitt B. McCloskey, Jr., as the constant taste tester (just one more bite.....) Thanks for your critique of my food and your endless proofreading. To all of you, somehow 'thanks' doesn't seem enough.

I also want to thank the Book Club of Eagle Ridge for input and many friends who have read and re-read parts of this book. I want to thank my extended family for tasting many of my concoctions as I experimented on them.. God bless them and their taste buds.

I want to pay tribute to my father, who passed away in 1990 with an unfinished book on genealogy of our family. I had promised I would finish it for him, and I did. It gave me lots of practice for this project. And my mother, who taught me the fun of cooking and experimentation and whose many recipes I have included.

And lastly, I want to thank any and all neighbors and friends far and wide who shared their recipes and added many suggestions.

When I started compiling this book, I lived in New Jersey, then Pennsylvania.I now live in Florida, where the fruit is abundant. We grow our own oranges, lemons, and limes. The mangos are from neighbors. The sea grapes are from Naples and Estero beaches. This makes picking fruits and vegetables and creating recipes a joy. In other parts of the United States many markets carry produce from around the world, and most of them at your finger tips all year long.

Thank you all.

©Connie Hope — Mexican Guacamole Dip PG 19

PG 35 Honeydew Soup — ©Connie Hope

©Connie Hope — Crunchy Pea Salad PG 39

PG 71 Tomatillo-Celery Salsa — ©Connie Hope

©Connie Hope — Jalapeño Jelly and Cream Cheese Appetizer PG 16

Fruit Yogurt Pie PG 104 — ©Connie Hope

Introduction:

Food is something we all need to sustain us. It can taste just okay or it can taste great. Great tastes can be in the preparation and the combination of herbs and spices and the ingredients we choose to blend with the food. It is the combination that creates the flavor and causes our palates to water in anticipation. Just okay, is not acceptable. Tasting exceptional is the way to go!

I have loved to cook all my life. I can remember standing on a chair with my mother, Blanche, in her kitchen, adding this and that to a can of tomato soup to change the flavor and create my own concoctions. After fifty-plus years of adding to the entrée, I decided to pass them on to you.

In Addition ...to the Entrée emphasizes the idea that by taking something purchased in the store as 'quick meal,' you can add your own personal flair. You can enjoy food that seems as though you spent hours creating and cooking, when in reality you did it in a jiffy. Most of the recipes that I have included are ones you can add to a main meal to enhance the flavor and create something great. It is not just your strawberry jelly or jam, but herb jelly or jam that would make the main dish tastier. I have included different salsas, chutneys, jellies, jams, and more to create a new savory treat. I have included instruction for canning some of the jellies and jams. It's not difficult. These also make great homemade gifts for the holidays and special occasions.

In today's busy life the 'cook' needs help. As we run home from work with no idea what to prepare, we know we want something special rather than mundane. Who has the time? You can stop at the market and pick up pre-cooked turkey breast, a roasted chicken or pork chops, and by adding a chutney, a relish or salsa, make a delicious and original meal with only a little preparation time. The preparation can be completed on a weekend or in an evening. Then on the way from work, all that is needed is a quick stop at the market. Voila! You have created a meal with pizzazz!

©Connie Hope

Black Bean Salsa pg 67 ©Connie Hope

Tomatillo-Celery Salsa pg 71

Even a selection of cold cuts with relishes or pickles or chutney really makes a ho-hum meal into a WOW lunch or dinner.

I have created and collected these recipes throughout my life wherever I have lived, visited, or traveled. They have come from friends, relatives, people I had met in my travels to St. Thomas, many islands in the British Virgins, the Windward Islands, Europe, and even just next door. I have used them, improved them, and sometimes I left them as they were. But, all are from the heart. It has been fun. I love to put fruits and vegetables together and create something new and intriguing. My own personal favorites are the chutneys and salsas. You'll notice I have a few more of them than other items. However, they do add that personal touch to a meal. Something to whet the palate and add ...to the entrée.

Enjoy!

Cucumber Relish pg 94 ©Connie Hope

Mango Salsa pg 70

Appetizers

An appetizer is a small portion of food served before the main meal. If there is an extended period of time from when your guests arrive and the meal is served, an appetizer will sustain the guest. The French version of appetizer is hors d'oeuvre. It is before the meal and consists of olives, celery, pickled beets, pickled mushrooms, sardines, and many other foods. Appetizers may be hot or cold and served with small plates or as finger food.

In my house the appetizer is a very important part of the ritual. We usually have a cocktail and appetizer to start off the evening. An hour later, the meal begins. I love making appetizers because there are so many choices. I have included a few of my favorites.

Baked Artichoke Appetizer

1 14 oz can artichokes hearts, cut in sections

2 **Tablespoons lemon juice**—*fresh is best*

1 **small white onion, diced**

2 **Tablespoons of Italian herb seasoning**

2 **tomatoes sliced thin** (*these are optional*)

6 oz **mozzarella shredded cheese** (*You can substitute either Monterey Jack or Provolone.*)

¼ **cup of parmesan cheese for the topping**

Splash of white wine

Sauté onion in olive oil until tender. Place in baking dish. Sprinkle with Italian herbs and splash of white wine. Place artichokes over the onion in baking dish. Place sliced tomatoes, optional, and shredded cheese on top. Bake at 350 degrees for 30 minutes or until golden. Remove from oven and sprinkle parmesan cheese on top. Place under broiler for 1-2 minutes until cheese is a little brown. Serve on small plates with forks. Serves 4-6

Baked Artichoke Appetizer ©Connie Hope

This is really great and easy. You can prepare ahead of time and heat it 30 minutes before your guests arrive.

Can also be served as a vegetable.

To make this recipe vegan, substitute the regular mozzarella with soy mozzarella cheese, and there is a 'soy and veggie' grated topping that is a substitute for parmesan cheese. *It is excellent!*

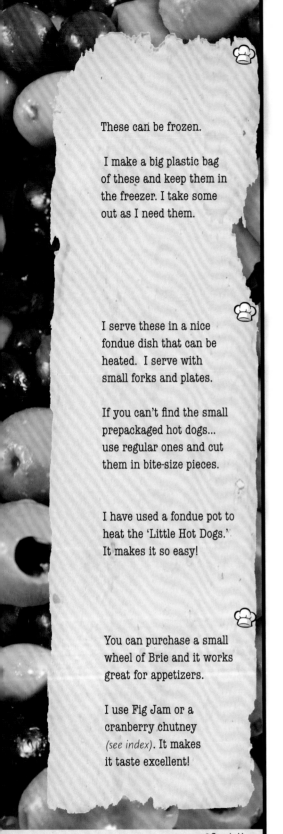

These can be frozen.

I make a big plastic bag of these and keep them in the freezer. I take some out as I need them.

I serve these in a nice fondue dish that can be heated. I serve with small forks and plates.

If you can't find the small prepackaged hot dogs... use regular ones and cut them in bite-size pieces.

I have used a fondue pot to heat the 'Little Hot Dogs.' It makes it so easy!

You can purchase a small wheel of Brie and it works great for appetizers.

I use Fig Jam or a cranberry chutney (see index). It makes it taste excellent!

©Connie Hope

Cheese-Olive Appetizers

2 cups grated sharp cheddar cheese

½ cup soft butter

1 cup sifted flour

Salt and pepper to taste

1 teaspoon paprika

48 olives, not real large (You can use either pimento-filled or not-filled olives)

Cream the cheese and butter together. Add flour, salt, pepper and paprika. Roll mixture into a small ball around the olives. Bake on cookie sheet at 400 degrees 15 minutes. Serves 4-6

Little Hot Dogs in Sauce

1 cup brown sugar

2 Tablespoons mustard

3 Tablespoons flour

1 can chunked pineapples (drain and save the juice)

1 cup pineapple juice

½ cup vinegar

1 Tablespoon soy sauce

1 pound miniature hot dogs

Mix everything together in a pot except the pineapple and the hot dogs. Bring to a boil for about 3-4 minutes, stir continually. Add the hot dogs and pineapple. Can be refrigerated until time to serve. Then reheat and place in a fancy dish or bowl. Serves 4-6

Baked Brie

1 small wheel Brie (or a section of Brie)

1 package ready pie crust

Any kind of jelly or jam or preserve (see jelly or jam sections)

Place one ready pie crust in a baking dish. Place Brie on top of crust. Spread Brie with jam or jelly on top and sides. Place second pie crust over the top and crimp sides to seal. If it is too large, trim edges. Bake 450 degrees for 12-14 minutes (should be golden). Serve with crackers. Serves 4-6

Salmon Mousse with Sour Cream Dill Sauce

2 cans salmon

¼ cup cold water

½ cup boiling water

1 envelop unflavored gelatin

1 teaspoon grated onion

½ cup mayonnaise

½ cup heavy cream

1 Tablespoon lemon juice

½ teaspoon tabasco sauce

¼ teaspoon paprika

1 Tablespoon chopped capers

2 cups cottage cheese, fine curd

Salt and pepper to taste

Soften the gelatin in cold water. Add the boiling water and stir until gelatin is dissolved and let cool. Add the mayonnaise, lemon juice, onion, tabasco, paprika, salt and pepper, and mix well. Chill. Add the salmon and capers and beat well. Whip cream and fold into the salmon mixture. Put into an oiled fish mold. Add cottage cheese to fill the mold and mix gently. Chill to set. Un-mold on a serving platter and garnish with watercress and lemon slices. Pour sour cream dill sauce over top *(see recipe below)*. Decorate with crackers or small slices of rye bread. Serves 8-10.

Sour Cream Dill Sauce

1 egg

Salt and pepper to taste

Dash of sugar

4 teaspoons lemon juice

1 teaspoon grated onion

2 Tablespoons cut dill

1 ½ cups sour cream

Beat the egg until fluffy and add lemon. Add remaining ingredients and blend in the sour cream last. Stir until blended and chill. Pour on top of Salmon mold.

Thanks Aunt Jane, for your recipe.

This recipe is great at a cocktail party or with many guests. It makes an excellent presentation.

©Connie Hope

This is something that looks different, but it tastes wonderful. *Everyone loves it!*

Marinade for scallops:
Marinate scallops for a few hours in:
1 juice of lemon
2-3 Tablespoons olive oil
Salt and pepper to taste

This appetizer is easy to create.
I microwave the bacon for a few minutes or use pre-cooked bacon.

This recipe is very easy to double if you need more.

You can freeze the asparagus rolls, and when you are ready to use them at your party, defrost and bake at 400 degrees for 15 minutes. They are great!

Hearts of Celery Appetizer

A full heart of celery

1 container smoked salmon and cream cheese or chives cream cheese

Keeping the celery as a whole and cut very ends off each piece of celery with the leaves. Open celery carefully and fill with cream cheese mix. When finished filling, tie with a string. Chill. Slice down each piece and put on a plate. Serves 6-8

Bacon Wrapped Scallops

1 pound of sea scallops (about 12-13)

6 slices partially cooked bacon (not fatty, smoked is good)

Toothpicks

Wrap each scallop in ½ strip of partially cooked bacon. Keep the bacon on the scallop with a toothpick. Place on broiler pan. Broil until scallops turn opaque and golden brown and bacon is done (about 6-8 minutes). Turn after about 3-4 minutes. Serves 4-6

Asparagus Spears

1 loaf thin bread—remove crust

3 oz package of bleu cheese

8 oz cream cheese

1 egg

2 packages frozen asparagus spears

1 stick butter or margarine, melted

Cook asparagus and drain. Cool on paper towel. Roll bread out flat with a rolling pin. Blend cheese, bleu cheese and cream cheese with egg. Spread mixture on bread. 1 piece of asparagus per slice of bread. Lay asparagus on bread diagonally. Roll up. Melt butter, put on a saucer, dip the roll quickly in butter. Put on cookie sheet and freeze for 1 hour. Cut into bite size pieces on an angle. If using immediately, bake 400 degrees for 15 minutes. Serve on a pretty dish. Serves 6-8

©Connie Hope

Mushroom Cheese Appetizers

1 pound mushrooms, sliced and chopped

5 strips bacon, cooked crispy and crumbled

½ cup mayonnaise

½ cup sour cream

1/3 cup cheddar cheese, grated

Mix all ingredients together. Put in a square pan. Bake 30-35 minutes at 350 degrees. Cool and put in a fancy container. Serves 6-8

Mushroom Cheese Appetizers

©Connie Hope

You can substitute low-fat or non-fat mayonnaise, sour cream, and cream cheese in any of these recipes to hold down the calories.

Everyone loves this appetizer. When unexpected guests stop by, this is fast and easy to serve.

Serve with:
Melba Toast Crackers
Chips
Crackers

Cheese Bars

½ lb sharp cheese, grated

1 stick butter

1 large onion, chopped

1 ½ cups Bisquick®

1 cup milk

1 egg, lightly beaten

Sauté onions in ½ stick of butter. Allow to cool. Take ½ of the grated cheese and mix with onions. Put aside. Beat Bisquick® and eggs together. Mix onion mixture and pour into 8-inch greased square pan. Melt other ½ stick of butter. Pour over mixture. Put other ½ of grated cheese and sprinkle on top. Bake 350 degrees for ½ hour or until golden brown. Cool for 1 hour. Cut into small squares and serve. Serves 6-8

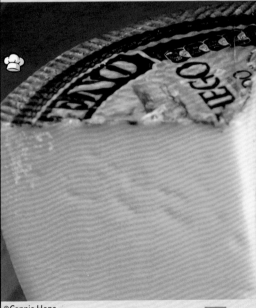

©Connie Hope

Jalapeno and Cream Cheese

8 oz Cream Cheese

Jalapeno jelly *(see index)* **or purchase from jelly section**

Put cream cheese on a 'neat' dish.
5-6 Spoons full of jalapeno jelly to cover the top. (see index)
Serve with small knife and crackers. Serves 6-8

Jalapeno and Cream Cheese   ©Connie Hope

Clams Casino

2 cans chopped clams

2 Tablespoons olive oil

½ cup minced onion

¼ cup green pepper, chopped

2 cloves garlic, minced

¾ cup bread crumbs

5 slices bacon *(use bacon that is not fatty)*

½ teaspoon dried oregano

2 Tablespoons grated parmesan cheese

2 teaspoon dried parsley *(or 2 Tablespoons fresh parsley)*

¼ teaspoon paprika for appearance

2 Tablespoons olive oil for drizzling

Cook bacon in microwave until crispy. Crumble, set aside. Put 2 Tablespoons olive oil in a pan and sauté onions, peppers, garlic until tender. In a medium size bowl add bread crumbs, bacon, oregano, cheese, chopped clams and the sautéed vegetables. Mix well and fill a clam shell or baking shell with mixture. Place on baking sheet. Sprinkle with parsley and paprika and drizzle with olive oil. Bake 450 degrees for 7-8 minutes. Serves 6-8

Dips

A dip or a dipping sauce is used to add flavor to raw vegetables, cubed pieces of meat and cheese, tortilla chips, and potato chips to name a few. Unlike other sauces that are applied to food, the dip usually has something put into it or dipped (hence the name dip or dipping sauce). Dips can vary from chocolates sauces and other sweets to beef bouillon, soy sauces, and sour cream mixtures. Dips are known mostly for use with finger foods.

I keep a container of sour cream in my refrigerator and have powdered soup mixes available. You never know when someone is going to stop by and you need a quick food to serve. The dip is that food. Dips are quick and easy appetizer recipes that can be created in minutes using common ingredients in your refrigerator and kitchen.

©Connie Hope

Hummus Dip *(Basic)*

1 can (15 oz) of garbanzo beans, drained, but reserve ¼ cup of liquid.

1/3 cup tahini *(sesame seed butter/paste)*

¼ cup orange or lemon juice

2 cloves garlic, pressed or minced

1 green onion, chopped or ¼ cup chopped chives

½ teaspoon ground cumin

Salt and fresh pepper to taste

Place all ingredients in a food processor or blender. Blend until smooth. Add bean liquid if needed. Serves 6-8

Variation for Hummus:

- Add 1 cup canned artichoke hearts
- Add 1 Tablespoon curry powder
- Add 3-4 more cloves of garlic
- Add 3-4 green onions
- Add ½ cup green or black olives
- Add 1 cup fresh basil leaves
- Add two roasted red peppers, purchased jar
- Add ½ cup fresh spinach
- Add ½ cup fresh spinach, 2-3 oz feta cheese
- Add 3 Tablespoons oil packed sun-dried tomatoes
- Use your imagination!

Hummus has become popular in the last 10 years. It can also be purchased in a tub at the supermarkets. This will save time.

Adding these fresh variations to a store bought hummus gives the illusion of being homemade.

I'll never tell!

This is one of my mother's favorite quick recipes. She passed this one on to me.

Thanks, Mom.

Thanks again, Mom.

©Connie Hope

This dip can be made ahead of time and put in the oven just before your guests arrive. It tastes like you spent a lot of time whipping it up. But it was quick and easy.

Spinach Dip

1 frozen, drained chopped spinach

1 package dried vegetable soup mix

1 can water chestnuts, drained and minced

1 cup sour cream

Dash of Worcestershire sauce or Tabasco sauce

Combine all ingredients. Refrigerate overnight. Serve with chips or melba toast. Serves 6-8

Shrimp-Dill Dip

1 8 oz package cream cheese, softened

¼ cup sour cream

2 Tablespoons lemon juice

2 Tablespoons finely chopped onions

1 teaspoon dill weed

¼ teaspoon Tabasco

1 cup chopped shrimp *(use either fresh or canned)*

Combine all ingredients. Chill for several hours before serving. Use with raw vegetables or crackers. Serves 6-8

Hot Crab Dip

4 cans white crab meat, drained

8 oz cream cheese, softened

½ cup mayonnaise

1/3 cup white wine

2 Tablespoons brown mustard

2 Tablespoons powdered sugar

2 Tablespoons onions, minced

½ cup scallion tips, chopped

½ cup artichokes, chopped

Preheat oven to 350 degrees. Soften cream cheese. Combine all ingredients except crab. Mix. Fold in crab. Put in casserole. Bake 15-30 minutes. Allow to rest about 10 minutes. Serve with hard crackers or bread. Serves 6-8

Guacamole Dip

2 avocados, peeled

1/3 cup onion, finely chopped

½ jalapeno chile pepper, finely chopped

1 clove garlic, chopped

1 medium tomato, peeled and chunked in small pieces

Juice of one lime

1 teaspoon sugar

Put avocados, onions, jalapeno peppers, tomato and lime juice in a food processor and pulse until blended. Add the chopped garlic. Add sugar. Put in a glass bowl. Serve with bowl-shaped corn chips. Serves 6-8

Mexican Guacamole Dip   ©Connie Hope

Mexican Guacamole Dip

½ can refried beans

½ cup sour cream

1 medium tomato, peeled and chunked in small pieces

¼ cup mozzarella cheese

Guacamole Dip from above

Layer each ingredient in a 2 to 3 inch deep glass bowl. Spread the refried beans. Use the guacamole dip from above. Spread the sour cream. Top with chunked tomato. Add mozzarella cheese to top. Serve with bowl-shaped corn chips. Serves 6-8

Mexican Guacamole Dip   ©Connie Hope

Connie's Cooking Tips:

©Connie Hope

■ What is tahini? It is used in hummus. It a paste made from ground sesame seeds. It is used in many Middle Eastern or Indian dishes. Most supermarkets or specialty stores such as Whole Foods or Fresh Foods carry it. But if you can't find it to put in your hummus, it will be fine without it.

■ To try to retain the green color of an artichoke when you are cooking it, add a small amount of lemon juice to the water.

■ You can sauté salad greens like lettuce, radicchio and others. Sauté as you would spinach. Cook quickly in a little olive oil, maybe some roasted garlic and salt and pepper. They make an excellent side dish.

■ Sometimes when you are cooking cauliflower, it will change its color. To slow this process, just add a little milk to the boiling water.

■ I usually steam my vegetables as it lets them retain more of their nutrition. A steamer is a folding platform that sits on the bottom of most pots. You don't boil your vegetables, but the rack allows the stream to wrap around them. Don't over cook, they are much better crispy.

■ Do not wash mushrooms under the water. Just wipe them off with a damp rag or use a mushroom scrub. Mushrooms are porous and will absorb some of the water.

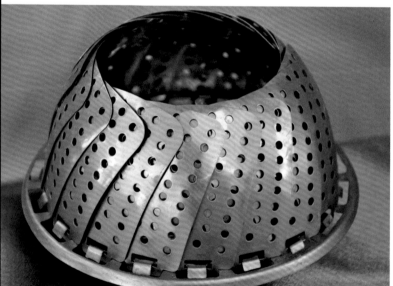

Spreads

are anything that you can puree to a smooth consistency and put on crackers, breads or vegetables and other food items.

Crispy Cucumber Spread

8 oz cream cheese, softened

½ cup buttermilk (1 teaspoon grated onions)

¼ teaspoon Worcestershire sauce

1/3 cup peeled and finely chopped cucumber

Combine first 4 ingredients. Mix until well blended and smooth. Stir in cucumbers. Chill for several hours. Serves 6-8

Salmon Spread

¼ cup plain yogurt

3-4 Tablespoons mayonnaise

1 Tablespoon minced onions, fine

¼ Tablespoon dill weed

¼ Tablespoon dry mustard

1 can salmon

¼ cup chopped celery

1 hard boiled egg, chopped

Mix yogurt, mayonnaise, onion, dill and mustard. Fold in the salmon, celery, and chopped egg. Refrigerate for several hours before serving. Serves 6-8

Feta and Cream Cheese Spread

2(8 oz) package cream cheese, softened

1 (8 oz) package feta cheese, crumbled

3-4 garlic cloves, peeled and minced fine

2 Tablespoon fresh dill, chopped

In the food processor, blend cream cheese, feta cheese, garlic, and dill. Put in a serving bowl and refrigerate for several hours before serving. Serves 6-8

Serve with:
Fresh steamed veggies
Fish
Pumpkin Soup -a dollop of spread in the center of the bowl of soup.

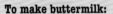

To make buttermilk:
Add 1 Tablespoon of lemon juice to milk let stand 5-10 minutes. You can substitute sour cream or yogurt.

Hummus is also a type of spread. I have it listed under Appetizers. Check it out there.

You can substitute Bleu Cheese or others for the feta cheese.

Serve on:
Melba toast
Crunchy bread
Celery
Broccoli

You can put in different olives or one kind.
Experiment and have fun.

You can add 1 anchovy fillet to this and/or 2 Tablespoons of capers

You can also add 2-3 Tablespoons of lemon juice.

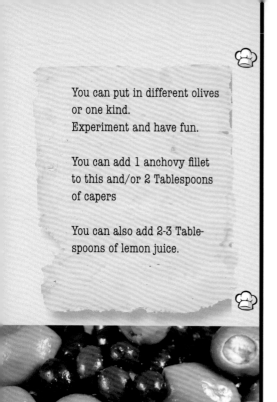

©Connie Hope

Serve any of these spreads with:
Crackers
Melba Toast
Small pieces of crusty bread

©Connie Hope

Olive Spread

1 cup pitted black olives

1 cup pitted green olives

1 cup pitted kalamata olives *(or use your favorite)*

2-3 cloves of garlic

3 Tablespoons of olive oil

3 Tablespoons of balsamic vinegar

Combine all olives and garlic in a food processor. Pulsate food processor. Add olive oil and balsamic vinegar. Pulse until smooth texture. Refrigerate for at least 1 hour before serving. Serves 4-6

Creamy Olive Spread

2 packages of cream cheese, 8 oz each, softened

1 cup chopped black olives

½ cup chopped pimiento-stuffed olives

2 cloves of garlic, minced

2 Tablespoons olive oil

2 Tablespoons lemon juice, *(fresh is best)*

Salt and pepper to taste

Mix all ingredients together until smooth. Refrigerate one hour before serving. Serve on crackers of your choice. Serves 6-8

Greek Olive Spread

1 cup sour cream

8 oz cream cheese

4 oz crumbled feta cheese

¼ cup lemon juice *(fresh is best)*

1 cup olive oil

2 cloves garlic, minced

½ teaspoon hot sauce

¼ cup green onions, minced

1 Tablespoon chopped parsley *(fresh is best)*

1/3 cup pitted olives – *use your favorite*

Combine olive oil, sour cream, lemon juice, garlic, and hot sauce in a food processor. Pulse for 30 seconds. Add cheeses and process until smooth. Put in a bowl and add remaining ingredients. Mix. Refrigerator one hour and serve. Serves 6-8

Apricot-Nut Spread

6-8 oz dried apricots
½ cup water
8 oz cream cheese, softened
½ cup nuts (use walnuts or pecans)

Soak apricots in water for several hours or overnight. Drain liquid except for 3 Tablespoons. Put apricots and 3 Tablespoons liquid in food processor and process for several seconds. Add cream cheese and process until smooth. Add nuts and process until smooth. Refrigerate. Serves 6-8

Carrot-Raisin Spread (or Dip)

1 8 oz package cream cheese, softened
½ cup grated carrots, packed *(use the largest hole on grater)*
(This is usually one large carrot.)
½ cup raisins, packed
½ cup nuts *(use either pecans or walnuts)* **finely chopped.**
Make sure you measure the amount of nuts after you have chopped them.
A little more in the recipe is better.
1-2 Tablespoons milk

Mix cream cheese, carrots and nuts in food processor until smooth. You may need to add 1-2 Tablespoons of milk to make smooth. Put in a bowl and hand mix raisins into cream cheese mix. Refrigerate until ready to serve. Serve in a small bowl with a spreader knife. Serves 6-8

Shrimp-Dill Spread (or Dip)

1 8 oz cream cheese, softened
¼ cup sour cream
2 Tablespoons lemon juice (fresh is best)
2 Tablespoons finely chopped onions
1 teaspoon dill weed, rounded on top
¼ teaspoon Tabasco
1 cup chopped shrimp

Mix ingredients in a bowl until smooth.
Serve in a small bowl with knife. Serves 6-8

Serve with:

Celery or other vegetables
Crackers
Crusty bread

Serve with:
Celery or other vegetables
Crackers
Crusty bread

This recipe can easily be cut in half.

*Thanks, Lisa,
for this recipe.*

Brief History of Cream Cheese

In 1872, cream cheese was invented by an American dairyman in Chester, New York. He accidentally developed a method of producing cream cheese while trying to reproduce a French cheese called Neufchatel. He started distributing his brand in foil wrappers in 1880 by the Empire Company. He called his cheese Philadelphia Brand Cream Cheese.

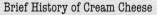

©Connie Hope

Connie's Cooking Tips:

■ A little information about 'the Olive.' There are green olives and black olives. Unripe olives are the green ones and fully ripe olives are black.

The olive is cured or pickled before eaten. There are several methods to do this. They are oil-cured, water-cured, brine-cured, dry-cured and lye-cured.

The green olive is soaked in a lye solution before the brine solution. The ripe black olives can go straight to the brining. Green olives are usually pitted and are often stuffed with fillings. Some of these fillings are almonds, capers, jalapenos, capers and my personal favorite, bleu cheese or feta.

Olives are graded into sizes such as small, medium, large, extra large, jumbo and the like.

They add a great deal to salads, spreads, dips, pizza, and many other dishes.

■ Never cook with any wine you wouldn't drink yourself.

■ Take some time and experiment with different herbs and vegetables. It is fun and you will find new taste treats. Try buying one new item each week and do some research on that item. You will increase your cooking knowledge and ability.

©Connie Hope

Soups

"I live on good soup, not on fine words"
Moliere—French writer 1622-1673

Soups are the greatest food to eat ...and to make. You have it 'In addition... to the Entrée.' People say, "I am a master of soups." In fact, I have joked that it will go on my tombstone, 'She liked to make all kinds of soups made with all kinds of ingredients.'

Soups can warm you when you are chilled or fill you if you are empty. There are hot soups and cold soups.

Soups should complement or contrast with what is to follow and usually fits in the following categories: bouillon, consommé, broths, jellied soups, vegetable soup, purees of vegetables and legumes, cream soups, bisques, chowders and fruit soups. Some of these are served hot, others are served chilled and some can be served either way.

I have included several of my favorite soups in this cook book, but someday I will create one of my soups. That could be endless.

Beet Soup or Borsch (sometimes seen as Borscht)

There are as many variations of this soup as there are serving plates for soups. They can be served hot or cold. I prefer hot.

½ cup carrot, chopped fine

1 cup onions, chopped fine

2 cups beets, cooked

2 cups beef stock—I like the stock in cans or boxes

1 cup very finely shredded cabbage

1 Tablespoon vinegar

Sour cream for topping

Put all ingredients in a pot and cover with boiling water. Simmer gently, covered, for 20 minutes then stirring. Add water if needed to cover and simmer 20 minutes more. Place in serving bowl. Add 1 dollop of sour cream to decorate top and serve with pumpernickel bread. Serves 4-6

Removing fat from soup

1. Chill the soup. The fat rises to the top and will solidify when cold. Use a large spoon and skim to remove it.

2. Float a paper towel on the surface of the soup. It will absorb a lot of the fat.

Some thickening ingredients for soup:
• Barley
• Rice
• Noodles and dumplings
• Cut potatoes
• 2 -3 Tablespoons flour or corn- starch added to 1 cup water.

Make sure you stir continually in the same direction so that you don't get lumps.

Borsch is a soup made mostly of beets. It was a specialty in Eastern Europe and Russia

Cooking Beets-Clean outside of beets and cut off ends. Place in enough water to cover. Boil for at least 30 minutes or until soft. Save the juice to make pickled eggs (see relishes and pickles). To remove skins, run beets under cold water. Hold in hands and the skin will pull right off.

Hubbard squash is another cultivar of butternut squash and is usually a 'tear-drop' shape. They are often used as a replacement for pumpkin

© Connie Hope

Hubbard Squash Soup (Butternut Squash Soup)

1 Tablespoon virgin olive oil

1 medium onion, diced fine

½ cup chopped scallions

2 garlic cloves, diced fine

1 quart vegetable broth, chicken broth or water

4 cups Hubbard squash or butternut squash, cubed and cooked
(2-3 squash)

1 teaspoon cinnamon

¼ teaspoon mace

Salt and pepper to taste

1 cup heavy cream (or soy milk thickened with flour and water) The cream is optional. I like it just as well without it.

Heat olive oil and sauté the onion, scallions, and garlic until golden. Add the broth and simmer 15-20 minutes. Add the squash, salt, cinnamon, pepper, and mace. Simmer for 15 more minutes. Put in food processor and puree. Add the heavy cream (or soy, optional). Continue to simmer until heated throughout. Garnish with chopped scallion, a dollop of sour cream or pesto (see index) or use your imagination. Serves 6-8

Hubbard Squash Soup (Butternut Squash Soup)

© Connie Hope

Squash & Carrot Soup

1 pound carrots-cleaned, peeled and cut into ½ inch slices

1 ½ pound squash, peeled, seeded and cut into 1 inch cubes *(You can use your favorite squash such as acorn, buttercup, butternut or any others)*

2 teaspoons of butter or margarine

½ cup finely chopped onion*(use either white onion or to give more color and a stronger taste use a Bermuda (purple) onion)*

1 Tablespoon ginger root, minced

1 ¼ cups cream *(use either half and half or light cream)*

1 cup chicken broth

2 teaspoons of grated orange zest

Salt and pepper to taste

Fill a soup pot with 2 inches of water. Add carrots and bring to a boil. Simmer for 10 minutes. Add squash cubes and simmer 10 minutes or until tender. Drain well and set aside. Put squash and carrots in food processor and puree. Melt butter in pot, add onions and ginger ,sauté for 2-3 minutes until onions are tender. Add carrots and squash in the pot with the onions. Add the half and half, broth, and orange peel. Bring the mixture to a boil, but do not let it boil. Reduce heat immediately or if electric, take off burner. Soup can be served hot or cold. Makes about 4 cups.

The orange and ginger add a great exotic flavor to the soup

You can put a dollop of pesto or sour cream to decorate the top of the soup.

It is a great soup to remove the chill in the fall air.

Broccoli Soup

1 ½ cups chicken broth

½ cup onions, yellow, chopped

Salt and pepper to taste

2 cup chopped broccoli

½ teaspoon dried thyme

1 bay leaf

Dash of garlic powder

Bring chicken broth, chopped onions, broccoli, and spices to a boil, then reduce. Simmer for 10 minutes. Remove bay leaf and puree soup in food processor. Make a white sauce * Slowly wire whisk into soup mixture until you have the soup to the consistency you desire. Heat slowly for 15 minutes, stir often. Makes 3-4 cups

*White sauce:

2 Tablespoons butter

2-3 Tablespoon flour

1 cup milk or half and half

Melt butter and slowly mix in flour to make a paste. Slowly add milk to flour mixture stirring with a wire whisk continually over warm heat. Always stir in the same direction. Mixture will thicken

This is a basic pumpkin soup recipe with a nice even and creamy taste.

See appendix for cutting and cooking pumpkin.

These soups can be served in a small, hollowed-out pumpkin. Cut off top of a small pumpkin down lower than usual. Save lid to keep soup warm. Use a melon baller to hollow out pumpkin to about ½ inch from skin.

Spanish pumpkin soup has a little more spice to the taste with the addition of the garlic and cilantro. It also is not creamy as there is not milk or cream added.

Pumpkin Soup

½ cup onions chopped

3 Tablespoons butter

2 cups mashed cooked pumpkin *(or canned, 20 oz can is over 3 cups)*

1 teaspoon salt

1 Tablespoon sugar

¼ teaspoon nutmeg

¼ teaspoon ground pepper

3 cups chicken broth

½ cup light cream *(can substitute soy milk and a little flour to thicken)*

Brown onions slowly in butter. Put mashed pumpkin into the onion pan and add salt, sugar, nutmeg and pepper. If you prefer a smooth soup, puree in food processor. Slowly add chicken broth, mixing with wire whisk. Heat thoroughly. Do not boil. Slowly add the cream and reheat. Garnish with croutons and parsley. Serves 4-5

Pumpkin Soup   ©Connie Hope

Spanish Pumpkin Soup

Add to the recipe of Pumpkin Soup

3 minced garlic cloves

1 ¼ cup cilantro, chopped

Remove the ½ cup cream

Bread cubes fried in garlic olive oil

Cilantro sprigs

Put garlic in with the onions to brown. Add cilantro with the chicken broth. Heat and serve. Garnish with croutons and cilantro. Serves 4-5

Pumpkin-Leek Soup

2½ cups leeks, use mostly the white part, diced

1 medium cooked, mashed pumpkin *(or 1 large can)*

1 can chicken broth (*10 ½ oz or use 1 ¼ cups*)

¼ cup heavy cream

1 teaspoon allspice, ground

½ teaspoon nutmeg, ground

½ teaspoon ginger, ground

¼ teaspoon cloves, ground *(this can be optional if clove is something you don't care for)*

¼ cup almonds *(toasted or blanched) (They are used for garnishing so I prefer the thinly sliced blanched, but your choice.)*

1 teaspoon cinnamon, ground

2 Tablespoons oil *(I usually use canola, but any will do.)*

Salt and pepper to taste

Several spoonfuls of sour cream for garnish

In a large sauce pan over medium heat, add the oil and leeks. Sauté until tender. Stir in all spices, broth, and pumpkin. Cover and reduce to a simmer. Simmer for at least 20 minutes. Stir occasionally. Put mixture in a food processor and blend. This may have to be done in several batches. Return the mixture to the sauce pan and heat. Season with salt and pepper to taste. Add heavy cream and warm until soup is heated thoroughly. Garnish with sliced almonds, sour cream or pesto. Makes 3-4 cups

Vegan Option

Omit the heavy cream. You can replace with soy milk, but you will have to thicken the milk a little with a mixture of 3 Tablespoons of flour and just enough water to make a thick paste. Make sure that you stir continually in the same direction with the wire whisk. Use Vegan sour cream for garnishing.

©Connie Hope

Baked Pumpkin Seeds
I worked with Eleanor and she gave me this recipe. Thanks.

The hardest thing is to get the fiber away from the seeds. Place seeds in a strainer and run water over. Pull the seeds away from the fibers with your hands. It is slimy.

Heat oven to 350 degrees.
Put seeds on a paper towel for a few minutes to remove extra moisture.

Spray a cookie sheet with nonstick butter spray.
Put the seeds in a single layer on the cookie sheet.
Sprinkle with salt.
Bake them for 10 minutes or until golden. Turn and bake another 10 minutes.
Cool and store in an airtight container.

Variation:
Try additional seasonings on your pumpkin seeds — either Cajun seasoning, Worcestershire sauce, soy sauce or garlic salt. These are some of the many possibilities.

This was my oldest son's favorite recipe to make when he was young. He would stand on a chair and put this together adding something new each time. You can do that too. Have fun and use your imagination.

My son would add:
½ cup red peppers to the sauté or Red bliss potatoes instead of regular potatoes.
Oregano
Basil

Use your imagination.

Great on a cold day and you need something to stick to your ribs.

Garnish with croutons, parsley, or paprika.

I serve the chowder with thick crusty breads.

Corn Chowder

2 cups corn (or off the cob) **drained, reserve liquid**

3 cups chicken stock or chicken cubes

Two separate ½ teaspoons sugar

½ cup onion, minced

¼ cup celery, minced

¼ cup butter

½ teaspoon dry mustard

Salt and pepper to taste

1 Tablespoon lemon juice (fresh is best)

1 ½ cups diced potatoes

3 drops Tabasco (or Gloria's West Indies Pepper Sauce, see index)

½ teaspoon Worcestershire sauce

Pinch thyme

Parsley to taste

Paprika

1 egg yolk-beaten

1 cup heavy cream (small container)

3 Tablespoons flour

3 Tablespoons milk

In a large pot put chicken stock, liquid from corn, ½ teaspoon sugar, and salt and pepper and simmer for 10-15 minutes. Sauté corn, onions and celery in butter adding mustard, ½ teaspoon of sugar and salt and pepper. Put sautéed mix in stock with lemon juice and potatoes. Allow to reach a slow boil. Cook until potatoes are tender. Turn down heat and add Tabasco and Worcestershire sauce. Wire whisk yolk and heavy cream in a bowl, then add ½ cup of the hot soup stock to the bowl and whisk. Add to the remaining soup. Serves 4-6 Make a thickening sauce with the 3 Tablespoons flour and milk and whisk into the soup slowly to thicken.

Corn Chowder   ©Connie Hope

Polish Meatball Cabbage Soup

2 heads cabbage-cut in quarter cuts then sliced thin

6 14 oz cans diced tomato or tomato sauce

1 large onion, chopped

3 Tablespoons lemon juice *(fresh is best)*

3 Tablespoons sugar

1 fresh tomato, cut in quarters

2 beef cubes in 1 cup boiling water

TO MAKE MEATBALLS:

2 pounds fat free ground meat *(or turkey ground meat)*

3 eggs

1 cup bread crumbs

½ cup cooked rice

Combine meatball ingredients and roll into meat balls. Heat in microwave until all the fat is out of them. I place them on paper towels. *(You can also purchase pre-made meatballs.)*

FOR SOUP:

Combine all ingredients except meatballs. Cook slowly for several hours. Add meatballs and cook for 1 hour more. Serves 6-8

Zucchini Soup

1 ½ pounds of zucchini

3 Tablespoons butter or margarine

1 small onion, chopped

1 teaspoon thyme

6 cups chicken stock

½ cup white rice, uncooked

Salt and pepper to taste

Grated parmesan cheese for top

Clean and cut off ends of zucchini. Grate. In a large pot, melt butter, add onions. Add zucchini and thyme, then heat for a few minutes. Add stock and rice and bring to a boil. Reduce heat and simmer for 30 minutes. You can puree this in a blender or serve as is. Serve with parmesan cheese on top. Serves 4-6

I worked with Betty Hutchins who gave me this recipe.

Thanks.
It is a tasty soup. Great for cold weather and lots of people.

This is warming with a grilled cheese sandwich on a cold day.

(Or if you are like me, I can have soup on a cold or a hot day. I love it!)

Gazpacho *(Cold)*

6 ripe tomatoes, peeled and chopped

1 purple onion, chopped fine

1 cucumber, peeled, seeded, chopped

1 sweet red bell pepper remove seeds and chopped

3 stalks celery, chopped

2 Tablespoons fresh parsley, chopped

2 Tablespoons fresh chive, chopped

2 cloves minced garlic

¼ cup red wine vinegar

¼ cup olive oil

2-3 Tablespoons fresh squeezed lemon juice

2 teaspoons sugar

Tabasco sauce to taste

1 teaspoon Worcestershire sauce

4 cups tomato juice

Salt and fresh pepper to taste

Combine all ingredients. Mix if you like things chunky or puree in food processor. Place in a tightly-sealed container in the refrigerator overnight to allow the flavors to blend. Serves 4-6

Gazpacho Soup *(variation)*

1 14 oz can tomatoes

1 large green pepper

1 clove garlic

½ cup olive oil

3 Tablespoons lemon juice (fresh is best)

3 cups beef stock

1 small Spanish onion, chopped (purple onion)

1 cup cucumber, peeled, diced

Salt and pepper to taste

Fresh, chopped 1/8 cup of any the following:

Chives   Parsley   Basil   Chervil   Tarragon

Or used dried, but not quite as much.

Add all ingredients together - leave it chunky or puree in food processor. Paprika for topping and a dollop of sour cream or fresh pesto *(see index)* on top. Refrigerate for several hours. Serves 4-6

You can add so many different spices to change the flavor:
Oregano
Thyme
Cilantro

I also have used beef or clam tomato juice for added flavor.

This is a quicker version by using canned tomatoes rather than fresh..

Check out the pesto in the index or use a jar of bought pesto for topping. Makes it interesting!

Pasta e Fagioli (pasta and beans)

Ham bone

Several slices of ham, chopped

3 Tablespoons of olive oil

1 ½ cups celery

1 cup onions, minced

1 bag (1 pound) Great Northern beans

3-4 cloves of garlic

½ teaspoon dried basil, dried oregano

2 Tablespoons chopped parsley

Salt and pepper to taste

4 cups chicken broth

Pasta *(about two cups cooked, but more is better)*

1 26 oz jar of spaghetti sauce

or use your homemade or use chopped or stewed tomatoes

Follow the instruction on the beans and soak 1 pound of beans overnight in 6-8 cups of water. Rinse beans and drain before using. Put olive oil in a large soup pot. Add the celery, onions and garlic sauté at low heat. Stir. When that is almost cooked, add the chopped ham. Add the chicken broth, the ham bone and the beans. Bring to a boil and then turn down to medium/low for 3 hours. Cook pasta separately, then add to soup. Add spaghetti sauce (or stewed or chopped tomatoes). Reheat to serve. Serve with crusty bread. Serves 6-8

You can easily double this recipe.

At Christmas and other holidays, I usually bake a ham. I always put the ham bone in a plastic bag and stick it in the freezer for future cooking.

The pasta for this soup is your choice. There are so many great ones. I also use leftover pasta if I have it. Bow ties (farfalle), small or medium shells, ditali, anelli (small rings), macaroni, penne, or spaghetti broken into thirds.

This was given to me by a friend many years ago. Maryanne was Italian and loved to cook soup. Thanks for the recipe. It is one of my most used.

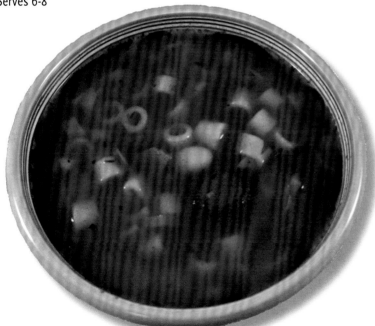

Pasta e Fagioli (pasta and beans)   ©Connie Hope

This has been a family favorite for many years. I save leftover vegetables for a few weeks in a container in the freezer, then make this soup. Or you can use fresh vegetables, canned, or frozen. It is tastes good and warms up the kids' tummies.

There is nothing that tastes better than a warm potato soup. Whether you like it with cheese or chunked potatoes or smoothly blended, it will always warm you and will always taste good.

Sometime I substitute chicken broth or vegetable broth for the water.

Variations:
Add ½ cup celery and ¼ teaspoon red pepper flakes to margarine and onions.
Or
Add 1 teaspoon dill weed with salt and pepper.
Or
Puree mixture before adding ham. This will make a smooth soup rather than the chunky.

Kitchen Sink Soup

1 pound lean chopped meat, cooked, and fat drained
1 cup each of any 4-5 of your favorite vegetables and any juice
(such as carrots, green beans, peas, wax beans, zucchini, lima beans)
1 cup pasta, cooked *(left over pasta is great)*
4 cups beef stock
Salt and pepper to taste
Dash of Tabasco sauce *or see Gloria's West Indies Pepper Sauce*

Combine everything in a large soup pot. Cook at medium heat until it starts to bubble. Turn low and simmer for 1 ½ hours. Serve with crusty bread. Serves 4-6

Potato Soup

3 large red potatoes, peeled, and cubed
2 ½ cups water
1 small onion, finely chopped
3 Tablespoons butter or margarine
3 Tablespoons flour
Salt and fresh pepper to taste
2 ½ cups milk
Pinch of sugar
1 cup ham, cubed
1 cup shredded cheddar cheese (optional)

Put 2 ½ cups water in pot, add potatoes and cook until tender. Drain potatoes and reserve liquid. Make sure liquid measures at least 1 cup. Set both aside. In a large pot, melt butter or margarine and add onion. Stir and cook until tender. Add flour and salt and pepper. Cook for 5 minutes. This will thicken the liquid. Add potatoes, reserved liquid, milk and sugar to onions in soup pot. Add the ham and cheese which are optional. Simmer over low heat for 30-40 minutes. Serve with crusty bread. Serves 4-6

Honeydew Soup *(Cold)*

1 cucumber *(If you use a hot house cucumber, it has no seeds or 2 regular cucumbers and scoop out the seeds with a teaspoon.)*

2 cups honeydew melon, chunked

8 oz plain nonfat yogurt

¼ cup fresh mint, cleaned

2 ½ Tablespoons fresh lime juice

Salt and pepper to taste

Mint leaf for decoration and a wedge of lime

Whirl all ingredients in a food processor or blender. Chill for several hours. Serves 4-6 Garnish with fresh mint and serve with a wedge of lime.

Honeydew Soup   ©Connie Hope

Perhaps this doesn't sound good, but it is a wonderful soup for warm weather or anytime. I went to a luncheon with my two long time friends. Bev served this soup and I just had to have the recipe. The only thing I did was add more lime. It was delicious!

Thanks, Bev

Split Pea Soup

1 pound green split peas *(in a bag)*

2 Tablespoons oil

10 cups of chicken broth or other vegetable/meat broth

3 small white onions, chopped

3 carrots diced

1 cup celery, chopped

Bay leaf

¼ cup parsley *(use less if you use dried)*

Salt and pepper to taste

Ham bone

3-4 pieces of ham, chopped

Wash and drain peas. Add oil in a large soup pot and sauté onions, carrots, celery. Simmer for 5 minutes until onions are transparent. Add the remaining ingredients and bring to a boil. Lower heat to simmer for 2 hours. If you like a smooth puree pea soup, put in the food processor or just leave it as it is. Serves 6-8

If I have cooked potatoes, ham or other vegetables, I save the liquid and use it in soups. I keep a plastic container in the freezer all the time for this reason.

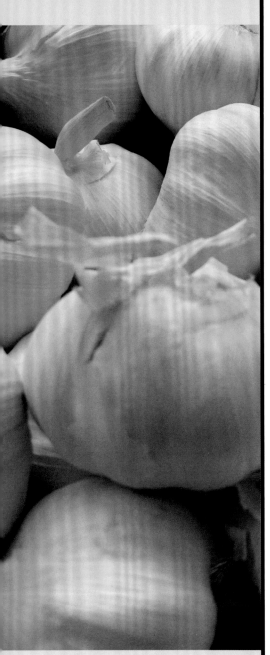

©Connie Hope

Connie's Cooking Tips:

■ How to make fat-free broth—

Chill your meat or chicken broth over night. The fat will rise to the top of the container. Remove the fat with a large spoon by gently skimming it on the top of the chilled broth. Then heat and use the broth for your recipe.

■ When you have finished cooking your dish, always taste it and adjust the spices and salt and pepper to your taste.

■ Microwave a lemon for 10-15 seconds before you squeeze it. This will increase the amount of juice.

■ Microwave garlic cloves for 10-15 seconds. It makes the removal of the skins much easier.

■ What to do with leftover wine that is only a small amount in a bottle? Put into an ice cube tray and freeze for use in casseroles and sauces in the future.

■ Substitution in a recipe—

If your recipe calls for water, try substituting juices, bouillon, or the liquid from cooking vegetables.

If your recipe calls for milk, try substituting buttermilk, yogurt, or sour cream. It adds a whole new flavor and sometimes improves nutrition.

■ To make buttermilk combine 1 Tablespoon vinegar to 1 cup milk and let stand for 1 hour.

Salads

There are hundreds of salads of all kinds. Some are with lettuce and vegetables. Those we all know and love. But many other kinds of salads are available. Some examples are main dish salads and side dish salads. Still others we know are pasta salad, potato salad, rice salad, and bean salads, as well as fruit salads and gelatin molded salads. We all know and enjoy macaroni or coleslaw salad. We use tuna, turkey, shrimp, chicken and others to make salads. The choices are endless and so are their names. Because this book is In Addition...to the Entrée, I have tried to use different types of salads that complement your main course.

Always wash your lettuce and vegetables before using. Run them underwater for some time to make sure they are free from spray-on chemicals. Put them on a paper towel to remove moisture. Today, there is even lettuce-cleaning spray at the market, and also a lettuce spinner.

Salads are served for lunch as well as dinner. They can be the main course or a side dish.

Some of the different types of greens for salad are:

Iceberg lettuce
Butterhead lettuce
Loose-leaf lettuce
Romaine lettuce
Red-leaf lettuce
Watercress
Spinach
Cabbage
White mustard leaves

I like this for lunch. You can also add pieces of chicken or turkey.

Blueberry Summer Salad   ©Connie Hope

Cool Blueberry Summer Salad for two

2 cups baby spinach leaves
¼ cup of blueberries
1 Tablespoon crumbled bleu cheese
1 or 2 Tablespoons low-fat balsamic vinaigrette *(to taste)*

Place spinach leaves in a low salad bowl. Add the blueberries, bleu cheese, and drizzle the salad dressing. Serves 2-3

This was my Aunt's favorite recipe. She always made it for family affairs. Thanks, Aunt Jane.

My girlfriend, Marcie, told me when she was in North Carolina they called this recipe 'Copper Pennies.'

Cut the carrots on the diagonal for a different effect.

Serve with:

This is great with any pork, ham, or steak.

I have used it for picnics and other outdoor events.

It is usually the hit of the event.

This was my mother, Blanche's, favorite recipe.

Thanks, Mom.

Aunt Jane's Carrot Salad

1 lb fresh carrots, cooked
(It is about 3-3 ½ cups or you can substitute 2 cans of carrots)

1 green pepper, chopped

1 medium onion , chopped

½ cup sugar

½ cup vegetable oil *(or olive oil)*

½ cup vinegar *(use your favorite)*

1 can tomato soup

Slice fresh carrots and cook until crisp. Mix the other ingredients, then add carrots last. Tastes better if it is made the day before. Serves 4-6

Aunt Jane's Carrot Salad   ©Connie Hope

Marinated Green Pea Salad

1/3 cup olive oil

2 Tablespoons red wine vinegar

Salt and pepper to taste

¼ teaspoon oregano leaves *(fresh or dried)*

¼ teaspoon basil leaves *(fresh or dried)*

3 green onions *(scallions)* **thinly sliced**

1 10 oz package frozen peas, thawed

1 cup thinly sliced celery

1 small green pepper, diced

2 medium tomatoes, cut in quarters

Lettuce leaves

Make the salad a day ahead. Mix first 6 ingredients. Add the peas, celery, and pepper. Use the tomatoes and lettuce for decoration. Serves 4-6

Crunchy Pea Salad

1 package frozen peas, thawed

1 cup celery, diced

1 cup cauliflower chopped

1 cup chopped cashews

¼ cup diced green onions

½ cup sour cream

1 cup ranch dressing

Crumbled bacon

Combine all ingredients. Chill for several hours. Serve on lettuce placed on individual plates. Garnish with tomatoes. Serves 4-5

Crunchy Pea Salad   ©Connie Hope

Serve with:
Steak
Chicken
Pork Chops
Hamburgers and hot dogs

This is my daughter, Jennifer's, recipe. She loves to serve this and does it so-o-o well.

The toasted seaweed can be purchased at most supermarkets; Whole Foods, Japanese or Chinese market, or other specialty stores.

Serve with:
Fish
Chicken
Baked Tofu

Japanese Sushi Salad

Sushi rice—make about two cups Follow the direction on the rice box. Chop in small pieces raw vegetables such as 1 avocado, 1 cucumber, diced carrots, baked tofu , or other vegetables. Toasted seaweed chopped in small strips. Combine all ingredients in a large bowl.
Saucy sauce—

1 Tablespoon tamari

¼ cup rice vinegar

¼ cup sesame oil

Brown rice syrup to taste for sweeteners
2 Tablespoons sesame seeds.
Put on the ingredients in a large bowl and toss to mix

©Connie Hope

This is a fun salad in the hot summer for lunch or serve for dinner with the protein additions.

Shrimp, chicken, or turkey can be added to this for protein.

Remember to wear gloves when cleaning peppers.

This can be used for other salads, too.

Asian Noodle Salad

1 package linguine noodles—cooked, rinsed and cooled

½ head Napa cabbage, sliced

½ head purple cabbage, sliced

1 bag baby spinach

1 red bell pepper, cored, sliced thin

1 yellow bell pepper, cored, sliced thin

1 orange bell pepper, cored, sliced thin

1 small container bean spouts

2 scallions, sliced thin

3 cucumbers, peeled, and sliced thin

1 bunch of cilantro-that will really add to the flavor
(I use ¾ of it in the salad and the other ¼ in the dressing)

1 cup whole cashews

Mix together and put in a large salad bowl.
Serves 4-6 *(large portions)*

Dressing

Juice of 1 lime

8 Tablespoons of virgin olive oil

2 Tablespoons sesame oil

6 Tablespoons soy sauce

1/3 cup brown sugar

3 Tablespoons fresh ginger, peeled and chopped

2 cloves garlic, chopped

2 small jalapeno peppers, chopped

Chopped cilantro, to taste

Whisk all ingredient in a bowl.
Pour over salad and serve.

©Connie Hope

©Connie Hope

Party Salad

½ 10 oz package fresh spinach, salt, pepper, and ½ teaspoon sugar

6 hard boiled eggs, finely chopped

½ pound boiled ham, cut in stripes

1 small iceberg lettuce, shredded, salt, pepper and ½ teaspoon sugar

1 package frozen peas, thawed but not cooked

1 medium red Bermuda onion, peeled and thinly sliced

1 cup sour cream

2 cups mayonnaise

6 oz Swiss cheese, shredded

8 strips of bacon, crisply cooked and crumbled

Important: Make sure everything is drained well.

Use a large clear glass bowl.
In the bottom spread the spinach.
Add a layer of hard boiled eggs.
Add a layer of cut-up ham.
Add a layer of shredded iceberg lettuce.
Scatter peas over all.

Pull onion slices into rings and spread on salad. Mix sour cream and mayonnaise together and spread on top. Arrange shredded cheese on top of mayonnaise mixture. Cover bowl with plastic and refrigerate overnight. Just before serving, sprinkle with bacon. Do Not Toss. Cut and serve portions all the way down to the bottom. Serves 8-10

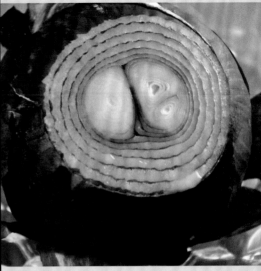

©Connie Hope

It is really a great tasting salad and looks nice on a buffet table.

A nice last minute company treat!

Variations:
½ cup fresh parsley
Or
2 teaspoons dill
Or
2 teaspoons Cajun spices

Shrimp Macaroni Salad

1 ½ lb cooked macaroni *(you can use any pasta you like)*

1 cup chopped celery

2 cans shrimp
(if fresh shrimp is used, you may need to cut them in half)

1 small onion, chopped fine

2-3 carrots, chopped fine

Salt and pepper to taste

Mayonnaise

2 medium tomatoes, chopped

Cook pasta and cool. Add remaining ingredients and a little mayonnaise at a time. Serves 4-6

Feta Cheese Pasta Salad

3 cups uncooked pasta *(your choice of size and shape)*

2 Tablespoons lemon juice

½ cup olive oil

Salt and pepper to taste

¼ teaspoon dried oregano

1 clove garlic, crushed

2 tomatoes cut in wedges

1 cucumber, peeled and sliced thin

1 green pepper sliced in thin strips

15 black olives

1 ¼ crumbled feta cheese

8-10 radishes, sliced thin

¼ cup green onions, sliced

2 Tablespoons fresh parsley, chopped

Cook pasta as per direction on package. Drain well and cool.
Combine dressing--oil, salt, pepper, oregano, lemon juice and garlic in small bowl. Wire whisk until blended. Combine pasta, tomato wedges, cucumbers, olives, green peppers, feta cheese, radishes, onions and parsley in large bowl. Pour dressing over salad and gently coat pasta. Serves 4-6

Sweet Cole Slaw with Caraway Seeds

1 large head cabbage, cut in quarters, then eighths

1 small yellow onion, chopped fine

½ cup shredded carrots, 1 medium carrot

Salt and pepper to taste

¾ cup mayonnaise, ¼ cup more

1 Tablespoon caraway seeds (optional)

2 Tablespoon cider vinegar

4 Tablespoons sugar

Cut cabbage fine *(can use a food processor)*. Add onions, carrots, salt, and pepper. Mix vinegar and sugar, then add ¾ cup mayonnaise and caraway seeds. Blend mixture into cabbage. Add the additional ¼ cup mayonnaise if you prefer moist and creamy. Serves 6-8

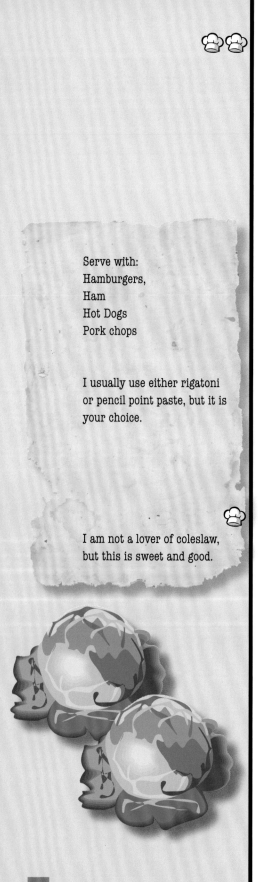

Serve with:
Hamburgers,
Ham
Hot Dogs
Pork chops

I usually use either rigatoni or pencil point paste, but it is your choice.

I am not a lover of coleslaw, but this is sweet and good.

Salad with fruit

2 cups lettuce greens of your choice

3 kiwis, skinned and sliced thin

1 cup raspberries, fresh or frozen

½ cup pecans, chopped

1 yellow bell pepper, chopped

½ cup yellow onion, chopped (optional)

½ cup of raspberry vinaigrette—use either store bought or homemade *

Put greens in a large salad bowl or on individual plate.
Add chopped yellow bell pepper, pecans and onion and toss.

Connie's Potato Salad

2-2 ½ pounds white potatoes (about ½ of a 5 pound bag)

¾ cup celery, chopped fine

¾ cup onion, chopped fine

¼ cup red pepper, chopped fine

½ cup olives, cut in half or more (optional)

Salt and pepper to taste

1 teaspoon sugar

Lime pepper (see appendix) Jane's Krazy Mix-Up Pepper ®

6-8 hard boiled eggs, shells removed

¼ cup fresh parsley

About 1 cup mayonnaise

¼ teaspoon celery seeds

Peel potatoes and boil while whole. Save the potato water for soup. Allow
the potatoes to cool for several hours, then cut in chunks. Add the celery,
onion, red pepper, sugar, and olives. Salt and pepper to taste. Cut eggs in
several pieces and add to potatoes. Add mayonnaise a little at a time to cover
mixture. May need more than the one cup. Serves 6-8 people.

Substitute strawberries or
other fruit you enjoy.

*Homemade Raspberry
   Vinaigrette

½ cup fresh or frozen
   raspberries
¼ cup apple cider vinegar
¼ cup balsamic vinegar
2 teaspoons sugar
1 Tablespoon mustard
   (optional)
¼ cup oil

Add all ingredients into a
food processor and puree.
Slowly add the oil from the
top until mixture is smooth.

I am known for my great tasting
potato salad. I hope you get as
many compliments as I do with
this recipe.

©Connie Hope

© Connie Hope

© Connie Hope

© Connie Hope

© Connie Hope

Connie's Cooking Tips:

■ If you can find fresh herbs, they are always better in a recipe.

■ Fresh herbs such as dill, chives, parsley, basil, etc, hold in small bunches and use kitchen scissors and snip at the ends. There are three good reasons to do this.

1. It is a lot faster than chopping them.
2. The herbs will be fluffier and not damaged.
3. Often when they are chopped, the leaves are damaged and seem wet.

■ Your refrigerator can be humid and is not recommended for storing herbs and spices for long periods at a time. Store them in a tightly sealed plastic container in your freezer. Remove a short time before you need to use them.

■ For dried herbs and spices, store in a cool, dark place. Again, the refrigerator is not a good place for dried herbs and spices. If you have a cabinet above your range, put them there. The warmth from the stove and oven will help to keep them dry.

■ Rule of thumb for dried herbs in proportion to fresh. Use about 1/3 of your dried herbs as it calls for fresh. The recipe calls for 1 cup of an fresh herb, you would use 1/3 cup of a dried herb.

■ Some spices are good to put on at the table by your guests. Some of these are black pepper, garlic powder, salt, and cayenne pepper.

■ Some spices go exceptionally well with sweet items. They are cinnamon, nutmeg, clove, and allspice to name a few.

■ Apples and avocados are natural ripening agents. If you put either in a paper bag with an unripened fruit or vegetable, it will help to ripen it.

Squash 101

The word 'Squash' is derived from 'askutasquash,' which literally means 'a green thing eaten raw' in the language of the Nahahiganseck Sovereign Nation. These are Native Americans who lived in the Narragansett Bay, Rhode Island, Connecticut, and Massachusetts areas and down into other states on the eastern shores. Squash was one of 'The Three Sisters'* planted by these native Americans.

Some squash can be eaten raw, while others are cooked. They can be pureed for soups, cakes, pies, and breads or sautéed, steamed, boiled, baked, and fried. However, squash are really fruit. Fruit have seeds on the inside as a tomato, but are used as a vegetable. In addition to the flesh, other parts of the plant are edible. The squash seeds **can be eaten or they can be ground into paste or pressed for vegetable oil. The shoots and leaves can be eaten as greens and the blossoms are good in cooking.

Squash have a nutritional plus. They are low in calories and have 20% of the recommended daily magnesium, potassium, vitamin A, C, E, fiber and calcium. They are also high in antioxidant and beta carotene, and are fat free and cholesterol free. Wow! All in one vegetable (or fruit)!

Squash can be categorized into two groupings: summer squash and winter squash. It is designated more by durability than by the harvesting time. Summer squash is thin skinned and bruises easily. The smaller, the more tender and sweet. Summer squash contains more water then a winter squash. Zucchini is an example of thin-skinned summer squash and will become soft and start to rot within a week. Winter squash is harvested fully mature in September and October and widely available until late winter. Winter squash has a hard, thick rind with the stem attached and is heavy for its size. You might even need a hammer and knife to penetrate the thick skin. But this skin helps make them remain durable for a long period of time. There are so many squashes it is hard to tell them apart. Here are just a few points on several of the most popular.

*'The Three Sisters' were the three main plants used for agriculture by the Native Americans: corn (maize), beans, and squash. They were planted together.

The cornstalks provided support for the climbing beans and shade for the squash. The squash vines provided ground cover to prevent weeds, and the beans provided nitrogen for all three crops.

**

I have given you a tip about pumpkin seeds and baking them. You can also use acorn, butternut, and other squash for appetizers and garnish by baking them the same way in the oven. See index for pumpkin seeds.

Summer Squash:

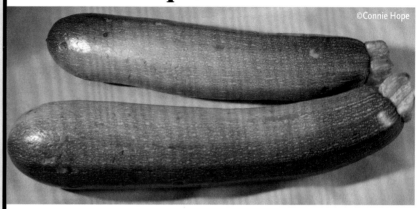

©Connie Hope

Zucchini is one of the most popular summer squashes and is often paired with its cousin, yellow squash. It is mild in flavor and can be eaten raw, grilled, fried, sautéed, baked, tossed in salads, and used in breads and cakes. Look for a glossy, firm, dark green skin when purchasing zucchini. The flowering tip of the zucchini, the blossom, is considered a gourmet delicacy. It is served as a side dish, sautéed or fried.

©Connie Hope

Yellow Squash like the zucchini is thin skinned, does not need peeling, and is tender and mildly sweet. There are a number of varieties including crookneck, straight neck, and yellow zucchini. Their names really explain their appearance.

Winter Squash:

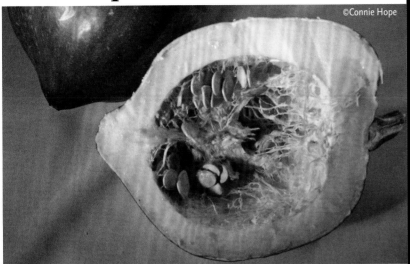

©Connie Hope

Acorn Squash is naturally sweet, slightly fibrous and can be interchanged in recipes with the buttercup squash. As its name suggests it is shaped like an acorn. Its distinct ribs run the length of the hard, blackish-green skin. It is not as difficult as some to cut in half for baking and filling with butter and spices. It is great pureed, roasted, baked, or used in soups, as main dishes, side dishes, breads and cakes.

Banana Squash is in the shape of a log or a banana and has a pale cream or peach exterior. It is not found in most supermarkets.

©Connie Hope

Buttercup Squash is squatty and green with vertical gray or light green stripes. It is decorative and has a tender orange flesh that tastes similar to a sweet potato.

©Connie Hope

Butternut Squash is a creamy-colored gourd-shaped squash that is one of the more popular varieties. It has a slightly nuttier taste. It has a thinner skin than most winter squashes and bakes well.

Delicata, Gold Nugget, Kabocha, Carnival, Autumn Cup, Ambercup, and Turban are harder to find and are not as popular.

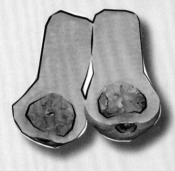

©Connie Hope

Hubbard squash are medium size and irregularly teardrop shaped with a skin that can have warts. They are blue gray in color with a taper at the end. Like all winter squash, the skin is not edible, seeds must be scooped out and the flesh is dense. Hubbard squash could successfully be stored for up to six months. The fibrous flesh is best baked and then pureed.

There are two sources for its name and origin according to Wikipedia. The first source states the name comes from Bela Hubbard, settler of Randolph Township, Ohio, in the Connecticut Western Reserve. The second source states that the Hubbard squash (at the time nameless) came to Marblehead, Mass. through Captain Knott Martin. A woman named Elizabeth Hubbard brought the vegetable to the attention of her neighbor, a seed trader named James Gregory. Mr. Gregory subsequently introduced it to the market using Mrs. Hubbard's name.

©Connie Hope

Pumpkin squash are mostly ornamental. Most people who cook or bake with pumpkins used the canned variety because cutting and preparing pumpkin is time consuming. I have written a section in the appendix 'Cutting and Baking a Pumpkin' for those who, like me, enjoy the challenge. You need to do something with all that leftover pumpkin after you have hollowed out your Jack-o-Lantern.

©Connie Hope

Spaghetti Squash is oblong and known for its separation into long, blond spaghetti-like strands when cooked. It has a mild, nutlike flavor. The yellower the outside of the squash, the riper it is. When cooked, the strands are used in salads, casseroles, or with sauce.

To prepare spaghetti squash, cut in half lengthwise and remove the seeds. Bake or boil until tender or microwave with plastic wrap for 12-14 minutes, testing softness. Then use a fork to rake out the strands and serve.

©Connie Hope

©Connie Hope

©Connie Hope

Connie's Cooking Tips:

- Squash is considered a vegetable by most people even though it is the "fruit" of the squash plant.

- Gourds are the inedible fruit. They have an extremely hard shell. When dried, they are used for decoration, vessels for water, storage containers or musical instruments. Very few gourds are used for consumption.

- The squash blossoms from summer and winter squash are edible. They are available from late spring to early fall in many markets. Choose blossoms that have closed buds. They will be somewhat limp, but this is normal. They do not keep very long. They can be eaten raw as garnish, in salads, battered and fried or stuffed and baked.

- Summer squash can be eaten rind, seeds, and all. The different varieties vary in size, shape, and color, but they can be used interchangeably in recipes. Select summer squash that's small and firm. They can be eaten raw as well as cooked.

- Winter squash, on the other hand, all have hard outer rinds that surround sweet, often orange flesh. They too come in many sizes and shapes, and they have a long shelf life, so they've long been a staple in winter and spring, when other vegetables are harder to come by. Unlike summer squash, winter squash must be cooked. They're usually baked or steamed, and sometimes puréed.

Vegetables and Starches
'Cheesie' Potatoes

6 medium potatoes, cooked, but firm

Salt and pepper to taste

½ cup melted butter or margarine

1/3 cup chopped onion

2 cups shredded cheddar cheese

1 pint sour cream

Let cooked potatoes cool. Then grate them into a bowl. Melt butter and add cheese. Fold into potatoes then add sour cream. At the same time, sauté onions in butter or margarine. Put into an 8 x 10 oven dish. If not cooking immediately, refrigerate. Bake at 350 degrees for 35 minutes. Serves 4-6

Thanks, Lee, for your potato recipe.

This can be made a day ahead and heated or frozen until needed. It's great!

This is a dish to take to someone's house.

©Connie Hope

'Cheesie' Potatoes   ©Connie Hope

Broccoli and Shells

1 pound shell pasta, cooked, and liquid reserved

2 packages frozen broccoli, cooked and drained

3 cloves of garlic, chopped

1 cup oil

3 envelopes chicken broth or chicken crystals

Cook shells, drain and reserve some of the liquid. Add oil and chopped garlic in a skillet, cook for 5 minutes. Put broccoli and oil mixture on top of shells in a bowl. Sprinkle with chicken broth and mix. If shells are a little dry, add some of the pasta water. Can be served hot or cold. Serves 6-8

You can always use two heads of fresh broccoli in this recipe.

You can also use cream of celery or cream of anything that sounds good to you.

Both of these recipes make a good dish for a buffet table or taking to someone's house.

It can be easily doubled if you need or want to make more.

Both of these recipes are good with:
Ham
Turkey
Pork Roast

This recipe is easily doubled. It seems to disappear quickly because so many people like it.

Spinach Soufflé

1 package frozen chopped spinach, defrosted and drained

1 can cream of mushroom soup (not diluted)

½ cup butter (margarine) melted

1 egg

1 cup croutons (these can be plain or herb)

2 oz grated mozzarella cheese

Mix all ingredients together. Put in casserole dish. Bake at 350 degrees for 50 minutes. Serves 4-6

Variations:

Substitute a package frozen asparagus
Substitute 1 cup mushrooms
Substitute 1 can corn
Substitute 1 can artichokes
Substitute 1 package frozen broccoli

Pineapple Soufflé

1 stick butter or margarine

1 cup sugar (or just a little less)

4 eggs, beaten

1 16 oz can pineapple, crushed and drained

4 slices white bread (cut off crust, break into pieces)

Cream butter and sugar. Add beaten eggs. Then fold in pineapple and bread. Put in casserole dish. Bake covered at 350 degrees for 45 minutes. Uncover and bake another 15 minutes. Serves 4-6

Artichoke Risotto

2 cups Risotto rice

1 cup dry white wine

6 cups chicken broth *(I like the chicken stock in a box)*

2 cans artichokes hearts, drained

¼ cup butter

3 Tablespoon olive oil

½ Vidalia onion, finely chopped

3-4 cloves garlic, minced

6 Tablespoons grated parmesan cheese

Salt and fresh pepper to taste

Put the olive oil in a large pan and sauté onion and garlic until lightly browned. Add the rice to the pan and stir for 1 minute. Add the wine to the rice mix and cook for 8-10 minutes. Stir continually. Then turn heat down to a simmer. Add about 3 cups of chicken broth and artichokes. Cook stirring frequently and adding 1 cup at a time of the chicken broth. Cook until rice is tender, about 30-40 minutes. Stir in cheese and salt and fresh pepper to taste. Serve as soon as possible and keep warm in a covered casserole dish. Serves 8-10

Serve with:

Beef Tenderloin
Filet mignon
Pork
Fish

This is a good tasting recipe, but it does make a lot. So plan to have leftovers.

Artichoke Risotto   ©Connie Hope

This is a quick and easy recipe for those nights you don't get home on time.

Acorn Squash Baked

1 acorn squash

2 Tablespoons orange juice

2 Tablespoons honey

2 teaspoons butter or margarine

Dash of nutmeg

Preheat oven to 400 degrees. Wash outside squash and cut in half. Remove seeds and save if you'd like to bake them. *(see index on pumpkin seeds).* Place in a baking dish. Mix orange juice and honey. Add 1 teaspoon of margarine to each half of squash and then add the orange juice/honey mix. Sprinkle with nutmeg. Cover pan with aluminum foil and bake 30 minutes. Remove foil and bake another 30 minutes until squash is tender. Any squash can be substituted for the acorn. Serves 2-4

Squash Medley Fried

2 cups zucchini, cleaned and coarsely chopped

2 cups yellow summer squash, cleaned and coarsely chopped.

½ cup red pepper, chopped

½ cup green pepper, chopped

½ cup onion, chopped

Salt and pepper to taste

2 Tablespoons butter or margarine

6 bacon strips, fried and crumbled

Put margarine in frying pan, add onion, heat at medium for 2-3 minutes until onions are translucent. Add peppers and squashes and heat on medium for 5 minutes or until squash is tender. Add bacon and simmer for several minutes. Serve 2-4

Squash Medley-Baked using the Medley above

1 ½ cups shredded cheese (any kind of cheese)

2 tomatoes, chopped or 1 can stewed tomatoes

Put the above in a casserole dish and add tomatoes and layer with cheese. Bake 375 degrees for 20 minutes.

Potato and Pepper Casserole

1 red pepper, cut in large strips

1 yellow or orange pepper, cut in large strips

1 medium onion cut in large pieces

4 Tablespoons olive oil

Salt and pepper to taste

2 pounds red skin potatoes *(small, oval potatoes)*

Boil potatoes until they are still a little firm.* Put oil in pan, add onions and peppers. Keep lid on and stir often. Simmer slow for 5-8 minutes until onions are transparent and peppers are still crispy and coated with oil. Put potatoes in casserole, toss in onions and peppers. Bake at 350 degrees for 30-35 minutes. Serves 4-6

This is an easy recipe because it can be done the day before.

* Water from potatoes can be saved for soups. Put in container in freezer for a later recipe.

This can be done ahead of time and left in refrigerator until needed

Potato and Pepper Casserole   ©Connie Hope

Two Squash Bake

3 medium zucchini cut into ¼ inch diameter slices

3 medium yellow squash cut into ¼ inch diameter slices

1 medium yellow onion, chopped

1 pound mushrooms, cut

6 oz. shredded cheese *(your favorite, cheddar or provolone)*

3 Tablespoons butter or margarine

Steam squash for 5 minutes or until still crispy. Fry onions in 3 Tablespoons margarine for 2-3 minutes then add mushrooms and heat until soft. Combine squash and onion mix in a casserole. Salt and pepper to taste and add cheese to top. Bake for 35 minutes at 350 degrees. Serves 4-6

©Connie Hope

My son's partner makes these for us every Thanksgiving.

Thanks, Michele.

These can be prepared the day ahead and reheated.

Serve with:
Pork chops
Steak
Ham
Chicken

This is a fast vegetable to serve.

Roasted Brussels Spouts

1 ½ pounds Brussels sprouts, trimmed and extra leaves removed.

2 Tablespoons roasted garlic in a jar

3 Tablespoons olive oil

Another 3 Tablespoons of olive oil

1 ½ teaspoons lime pepper *(see appendix)* **or regular pepper**

Salt to taste

Preheat oven 400 degrees. Place Brussels sprouts, 3 Tablespoons oil, garlic, and pepper in a re-sealable plastic bag. Seal and shake to coat the Brussels sprouts thoroughly. Coat baking sheet with 3 Tablespoons of olive oil and place Brussels on baking sheet in the center of the oven. Roast for 5 minutes then turn and roast another 5 minutes, turn and roast another 5 minutes. The Brussels sprouts should be a dark brown roasted color. You may need to leave in for another 5 minutes. Serves 6-8

Roasted Brussels Spouts   ©Connie Hope

Spinach Fry

1 package baby spinach

2 Tablespoons roasted garlic in a jar

½ pound sliced mushrooms *(your favorite)*

Salt and pepper to taste

2 Tablespoons olive oil

Add olive oil to a deep sided pot. Heat on medium and add the mushrooms and garlic for several minutes until the mushrooms are tender. Add ½ package of spinach to mushroom and garlic. Put cover on and let heat for 1-2 minutes, stir several times. Remove cover and add remaining spinach and stir. Serves 3-4

Wild Rice Special

1 package wild rice

½ cup pecan pieces

1 cup dried cranberries

Follow the instructions on the wild rice package. When the rice is completed, add the pecans and cranberries. Reheat for a few minutes. Serves 4-6

Red Cabbage

3 cups red cabbage, chopped

1-2 Tablespoons olive oil

2 Tablespoons cider vinegar

1 Tablespoon sugar

Soak the chopped red cabbage in cold water for at least one hour. Heat oil in a skillet, drain the cabbage and put in skillet. Cover, and cook for 3 minutes on medium heat then stir. Repeat cooking for 3 minutes and then stir. Then stir in vinegar and sugar. Serves 4-6

Roasted Asparagus

1 pound asparagus, rinsed, trimmed, paper towel dried

3 Tablespoons olive oil

1 Tablespoon minced, roasted garlic in a jar

Salt and lime pepper (see appendix)

Preheat oven to 400 degrees. Put olive oil and garlic together. In a glass baking dish or cookie sheet, toss asparagus with the garlic/olive oil mixture. Salt and pepper to taste. Bake asparagus until tender and brown, 20-25 minutes, turning them at least twice. Remove and put on serving platter. Serves 4-6

©Connie Hope

Serve with:
Pork
Steak
Chicken
Fish

This is so quick and easy when you are having company and want to have a colorful table.

You can substitute cherries, blueberries, or other fruits into the rice.

Serve with:
Pork
Ham
Sausage

Serve with:
Meat loaf
Steak
Chicken
Ham
Pork

Connie's Cooking Tips:

- To keep potatoes from getting buds, place an apple in the bag with them.

- One utensil I recommend is a potato ricer for mashing potatoes. It looks something like a giant garlic press, and is inexpensive. It makes great fluffy mashed potatoes. There are many other uses.

- Tomatoes don't ripen faster in sunlight. The warmth helps them ripen. Put them in a basket or bowl near your oven so they get the warmth. Also store with the stems downward, which helps them stay fresher.

- When cooking potatoes or most vegetables, always save the water. It is full of nutrients. I always keep a plastic container in my freezer and when I have cooked a vegetable, I transfer the liquid to the container and freeze. I use this for soups, stews or gravies that I will be making in the future. There is nothing more delicious than potato soup with the potato liquid or chicken soup with carrot liquid.

- To keep salt from clogging in the shaker in hot weather, add ½ to 1 teaspoon of uncooked rice to the shaker.

- Store freshly cut basil and parsley on your kitchen counter in a glass container. Make sure that the water level is only covering the stems and change the water occasionally. This will keep for several weeks and look and smell great on your counter. It may even develop roots. Basil does not like to be cold. Do not put it in the refrigerator because it will turn dark and rot and die.

Sauces

Some sauces complement the food and enhance the flavor. Some sauces are meant to be the dominant flavor. All sauces should be perfectly smooth like successful soups.

It is the sauce that can change a dish from mundane to spectacular. If you want to win a reputation as a good cook, learn to make and then add sauces to your dishes.

If you are adding wine to a recipe, make sure not to boil the sauce, as it will ruin the delicate flavor of the wine.

Be creative. Add pesto to soups and plum sauce to plain broiled chicken from the market. You are in charge and can create something extraordinary.

Red Wine Sauce

1 Tablespoon minced shallots
¾ cup red wine—I prefer a drier red wine
½ cup butter or margarine
2-3 teaspoons chopped parsley (fresh is best)
Salt and pepper to taste

Cook the shallots in wine in a small pot until liquid has been reduced to about ¼ cup. Remove from heat. Cream butter with parsley using an electric mixer. Gradually beat in the shallot-wine mixture. Salt and pepper to taste.

Sour Cream Horseradish Sauce

½ cup sour cream
2 Tablespoons horseradish *(I use more as I love that hot flavor)*
Salt and pepper to taste

Combine sour cream and horseradish and mix well. Salt and pepper to taste. Refrigerate until time to serve.

You can thicken sauces like you do soups. Use flour and water or cornstarch, barley, or rice.

Serve with:

Steak

Great with grilled steak, roast beef, or prime rib.

Serve with:

Steak, prime ribs, roast beef

I use a wire whisk to mix the sour cream and horseradish. In fact, I use a wire whisk to mix most of my sauces. It just makes it smoother and adds air as you are mixing.

I was given this recipe from the mother of one of our employees when I lived in St. Thomas. When I tasted the Pepper Sauce, I liked the very hot and spicy flavor and asked her for the recipe. I named it after the creator of the sauce.

This condiment is VERY HOT and should be used sparingly until you get used to it. It can be added to soups, stews, and curries. You can add to recipes that call for hot sauce or even hot peppers.

Most tables in the West Indies always have a bottle of this type of sauce.

I have seen recipes that use one ripe mango or papaya pureed. It adds to the thickness of the sauce, but I don't care for the flavor. But you might, so try it. Experiment....

Serve with:

Hamburger
Steak
Pork
Stew
Tofu
Quesadas

©Connie Hope

Gloria's West Indies Pepper Sauce

1 to 5 habanero chiles
½ cup cider vinegar or you can use malt vinegar
½ cup water
1 medium Vidalia onion, cut in chunks
1-2 cloves of garlic
Salt and fresh pepper to taste
1 inch piece of fresh ginger, peeled
½ Tablespoon honey
½ teaspoon turmeric
1 Tablespoon dry ground mustard
3 Tablespoons olive oil

Grind the peppers, onions, ginger, and garlic in a food processor or food chopper. Place in a glass bowl. Combine vinegar, water, and salt and pepper in a pot and bring to a boil for 1 minute. Pour boiling mix over pepper mixture. Allow to cool just a little. Slowly add olive oil, honey and spices and use a wire whisk.

Put in a glass sealable container. I use a 1 pint jar that has been cleaned with very hot water. Shake well. Let it sit in the refrigerator in the closed container for a few days. It will get spicier the longer you have it. It can be refrigerated for 6-8 weeks with the lid on tight.

I started out with only 1 habanero chili in this recipe, then I added a second and I've stayed there. But you can work your way up to 5 if you can take the heat. I like mine at 2 habanero chiles.

West Indies Pepper Sauce or Dip

1 pint cream
dried dill weed to taste
Add Gloria's West Indian Pepper Sauce to taste until you achieve just the right zest you want.

Combine ingredients. Mix until smooth.
Serve with corn chips or tortillas.

Lime Mustard Sauce

1/3 cup lime juice—Use either fresh squeezed lime or bottled lime juice.

2 cloves garlic—finely minced

1 habanera chili pepper—remove seeds and mince
(or you can use 1-2 teaspoons of Gloria's West Indies Pepper Sauce)

¼ cup mustard—Dijon style or stone mustard tastes best

2 Tablespoons mango chutney *(or Mango-Papaya Chutney or Mango-Ginger Chutney)* **See these recipes in index or purchase a jar at a store**

4 Tablespoons of honey.

Blend all ingredients together in a food processor until smooth. Add more honey for sweetness to your taste. Can be kept in the refrigerator for several days. Makes 1 -1 ½ pints

©Connie Hope

Lime Mustard Sauce

Cilantro Sauce

1/3 cup fresh cilantro, finely chopped

1 teaspoon lime juice (You can use key limes also)

1 teaspoon capers

1/3 cup sour cream

1/3 cup mayonnaise

Salt and peppers to taste

Dash of cayenne pepper or red pepper flakes

Combine all ingredients in a bowl. Mix well.
Refrigerator about 1 hour before serving.

Serve with:
Chicken
Fish
Turkey

When cutting and cleaning hot peppers, either wear rubber gloves to protect your hands or immediately upon completion wash hands in salt and water, then with soap.

There is nothing worse than rubbing your eyes or a cut on your fingers after working with hot peppers.

Trust me on this one!

Serve with:

Fish
Conch Fritters
Chicken fingers

©Connie Hope

This dip complements hot and spicy Indian dishes.

It is slightly salty and cool and will balance out the hot and spicy food.

* To remove the seeds from a cucumber use a teaspoon and scoop them out.

This will allow any excess water to drain.

See recipe in index for Plum jam.

Serve with:
Duck
Pork
Sliced beef strips

Yogurt Sauce or Dip

2½ cups plain low-fat yogurt

½ cucumber, peeled and seeded

1 ripe tomato, chopped

1 Tablespoon chopped cilantro-fresh

1 /2 teaspoon cumin seeds (toasted)

1 Tablespoon mint chopped—fresh *(I grow mint and spearmint in my garden and use both together or interchange each.)*

½ teaspoon salt

Use a coffee filter to strain 1 ½ cups plain low-fat yogurt. Allow the yogurt to drain for several hours to thicken. Mix in the other 1 cup of yogurt, not drained. Slice cucumber in half lengthwise. Scrape the seeds from each side.* Dice the cucumber into small pieces. Roast the cumin in a dry pan for a few minutes until brown. Add the cumin to the yogurt. Place all ingredients except the tomato, cilantro, and mint in a food processor. Blend for a minute. Fold in the chopped tomato, mint, and cilantro. Allow to cool in refrigerator for at least one hour. Serve with hot and spicy food or on thin crackers. Makes about 2 ½ cups

Plum Sauce

2 heaping Tablespoons plum jam (see index for recipe)

2 Tablespoons soy sauce

¼ teaspoon red pepper, or cayenne

1 teaspoon sesame oil (or olive oil)

¼ teaspoon grated ginger *(fresh is best, but can use jarred or canned)*

1 teaspoon rice vinegar

Cook the mixture until it bubbles (a slow boil). If mixture is very thin, you can make a cornstarch paste with a little water. Continue heating slowly for 2 minutes. Can be stored in the refrigerator for a week. Makes about ½ cup.

Salsa

Salsa is translated from Spanish as 'sauce.' It is used heavily in Mexican cooking. Salsa is perfect for summer eating and ideal for grilling and barbecuing food. There are salsas made with fruits and with vegetable. Some salsas are cooked, some are not. The most important element of a salsa is the freshness of the ingredients. Salsas bring color and variety to your plate. For years salsa was just referred to as the bowl of brightly colored fruits and vegetables that you put on a chip. No more. It has come of age and stands by itself. Salsa is easy to prepare, yet can create a ho hum dish into a great dish. Colorful and fresh chilies are finely chopped and combined with fruits, vegetables, and herbs to create an addition to simple dishes and meals ranging from fish to meat and vegetable to even the egg. Salsas range from hot, delicately spiced, sweet and sour or just hot and sweet. You are the cook and you can create what you want In Addition... to the Entrée. (see appendix for 'What Makes A Pepper Hot')

Chile Peppers

Chile peppers provide the basis of most salsas and are combined with an endless variety of other flavors. Some of the peppers and chilies used in either salsas or chutneys are very important. Today, we can get most of this either in our regular supermarket or a nearby specialty store.

Salsas that are red in color with either tomatoes or red chiles are typically called Salsa Roja. Salsas that are green are typically called Salsa Verde. The salsa verde is green because it is made from tomatillos or green chiles.

Many salsas improve in flavor when they have been refrigerated for several hours. The exception is any salsa that contains avocado. Adding lime juice helps stop the darkening of the avocado. However, the best remedy is to add the avocado just before you are serving it. And do not keep for a long period of time.

Most peppers are native to Central America, Mexico, and South American. They were given their name by Christopher Columbus and Spanish explorers who were searching for peppercorn plants that produce the spice, black pepper. Around 1492, Columbus and his explorers discovered sweet and hot peppers in the West Indies and took them back to Europe. The pepper quickly became a favorite food and spice throughout the world

Salsa is also a Latin dance.

Here's what to do. When you are cooking in the kitchen, dance the salsa and have fun with the preparation of the salsa.

Store sweet peppers unwashed in a plastic bag in the refrigerator for up to a week.

Store fresh hot peppers wrapped in a paper towel instead of plastic. They will keep longer that way.

©Connie Hope

Hot peppers add zest to any dish. They perk up pasta and charge up your jambalaya.

Have fun experimenting with different kinds.

I have listed several of the chili peppers used in many of my recipes.

Serrano Chiles

©Connie Hope

The Serrano pepper is pronounced: shu rah noh.

Serrano chili peppers have very thin walls. They don't need to be steamed or peeled before using. This makes it the easiest pepper to use for salsas. It is green in color at first then ripens to red, brown orange, or yellow. Serrano chili peppers do not dry well because they are meaty. The Serrano chile pepper is said to be about five times hotter than the jalapeno. Be careful not to put your fingers to your eyes when cutting them. Wearing gloves is a good idea. (see appendix for 'What Makes A Pepper Hot')

Habanero Peppers

©Connie Hope

The habanero is pronounced: hah bahn air oh.
The habanero is the hottest chili pepper you'll find in most grocery stores. They are very, very hot. The oil in the habanero chili pepper can be very painful if you get it in your eye. The best solution is to wear gloves when you prepare them. Unripened habanero are green, but the most common color of a mature habanero varies from orange to red, but sometimes white, brown and pink can be noticed.

Jalapeno Peppers

©Connie Hope

Jalapeno is pronounced: hah lah pain yo. Many people think that the jalapeno pepper is a very hot pepper when it is actually between mild to hot. The hottest part of the pepper is in the veins that dip into the seeds. If you want a milder pepper flavor, just remove these parts when following your recipe. This pepper is usually sold when it is still green. If the jalapeno is dried, it is called a chipotle. Handling fresh jalapenos may cause mild skin irritation, so always use gloves when cutting and cleaning them. (see appendix-'What Makes A Pepper Hot')

Tomatillos

©Connie Hope

Tomatillos is a relative of the tomato. It provides the tart flavor in many Mexican green sauces. In Mexico it is called 'tomates verde.' The fruit is 1 to 2 inches wide and has a papery outer skin which is peeled off when used. The tomatillo is actually used when it is green and they have a very tart flavor, not at all like a tomato. There is really no substitute for a tomatillo.

Cilantro

Cilantro, sometimes referred to as fresh coriander, is a green leafy herb found in your produce department. It has a very pungent flavor and looks a little like Italian flat leaf parsley. It can add so much to any of your favorite dish. It is my favorite spice.

Garlic

Garlic should have a tight head. The stronger garlic flavor is in the smaller cloves. When the cloves are too large, their flavor turns bitter. Garlic can be chopped, minced, or pressed to get the flavor.

Kiwi-Pineapple Salsa

½ fresh pineapple or one can pineapple, cut in small pieces

4 kiwis cut in small pieces

2 mangos semi-ripe, cut in small pieces

Slice of lemon

Anise to your taste. My taste is about ½ teaspoon

Cilantro- ½ cup of cilantro chopped fine *(just use the green tips—I put it in a blender and mix to fine consistency.)*

Cut all fruit into small pieces. Mix together. Put in a container that is air tight. Make at least 24 hours ahead. Refrigerate so the favors blend. Can be kept in refrigerator for several weeks.

©Connie Hope

Black Bean Salsa

Black Bean Salsa *(can also be called 'salad')*

1 15 oz can black beans, drained

1 15 oz can corn, drained

1 medium purple onion, chopped and diced (about 1 cup)

1 medium red bell pepper, chopped and diced (about 1 cup)

1 small can chick peas, drained (optional) OR

1 15 oz can dark kidney beans, drained and rinsed (optional)

½ cup packed cilantro, chopped (about one bunch)

Juice of 2 fresh limes

Salt and pepper to taste

Mix together all ingredients. Refrigerate. Flavor will enhance overnight. Serve next to your main dish. Serves 6-8.

Serve with:
Turkey
Ham
Fish
Pork Chops

©Connie Hope

Serve with
Chicken
Pork
Shrimp
Fish

I love the taste of the cilantro in this salad, so I sometimes add more, but you can decrease the amount if you choose.

I use a lime pepper made by Jane's Crazy Mixed-Up Lime Salt®.

It's the best.
See appendix.

See appendix for fruit squeezer. I used it to squeeze the lime juice.

Serve with:
Fish
Chicken
Shrimp

When traveling to Palm Island in the Windward Islands, a restaurant used this recipe. I asked the waiter if he could get me the recipe. The waiter spoke me the recipe as I wrote it on a napkin. Of course there weren't any amount of ingredients. I had to try and work it out. I've changed a few items. I prefer red onions and I have added more cilantro.

Serve with:
Chicken
Fish
Ham
Cheeses
Tofu

Avocado-Key Lime Salsa

2 ripe avocados, peeled and cubed
(I usually put lemon juice on the avocados so they don't darken)

3 key limes, peeled, seeded, and chopped

1 key lime for squeezing

1 red onion, diced

1 clove garlic, minced or finely chopped

1 teaspoon cumin

1 red bell pepper, diced

2-3 Tablespoons fresh cilantro, chopped

2 Tablespoons olive oil

Salt and pepper to taste

Combine all ingredients. Squeeze key lime over salsa. Refrigerate for one hour before serving. It does not stay fresh for any length of time. Serves 4-6

Orange Salsa

4 oranges, peeled, sectioned and cut in pieces
2 juice of limes
½ bunch of cilantro, chopped fine
2 red bell peppers, quartered, finely chopped
¼ cup olive oil
¼ cup pine nuts *(optional)*

Mix all ingredients together. Can be set aside and stored in refrigerator. Serves 4-6

Orange Salsa

Mango and Black Bean Salsa

1 ripe mango, cut in small pieces

¾ cup black beans

1 medium tomato, cut in small pieces

¾ cup red onion chopped in small pieces

1 medium red pepper chopped in small pieces

Juice from 1 lime

¼ cup brown rice vinegar

1 small jalapeño pepper cut in small pieces

½ cup mint *(fresh is best)*

Sea salt to taste

Black pepper to taste

Mix all ingredients together in a bowl. Refrigerate for several hours before using. This way the juices will intermingle. Can be refrigerated for several weeks.

Mango Salsa

1 ½ mangos, diced

½ red pepper, diced

½ yellow pepper, diced

15 oz can pineapple chunks

½ red onion, diced

salt and pepper to taste

¼ cup honey

¼ cup molasses

15 oz can black beans, rinsed and drained *(optional)*

Put 1/3 of the mango into the blender and puree. Combine with the remainder of the cubed mango. Stir in remaining ingredients. Refrigerate before serving. Can be refrigerated for several weeks.

Mango Salsa

Serve with:

Chips

Fish

Chicken

Remember, this has to be scooped on a chip, so cut cubes small and bite size.

When cutting a jalapeno pepper, always wear rubber gloves.

Cut the pepper in half, clean out and remove the seeds with a teaspoon.

I like this without the black beans, but either way is delicious.

This salsa is sweeter than most.
Serve with:
Fish
Chicken
Pork
Shrimp

©Connie Hope

Serve with:
Fish
Chicken
Shrimp

*See appendix on How to Cut a Mango

Remember to use gloves when cleaning hot peppers. If you want a hotter salsa leave the seeds in. I usually take them out, as it is too hot for my taste.

A neighbor in St. Thomas gave me this recipe. I have used it for many years. I love the taste of the cucumber.

Serve with:

Fish
Chicken
Shrimp

Mango Salsa variation

1 ripe mango,* peeled, pitted, and diced
½ jalapeño pepper, diced and remove seeds
¼ cup red onion, diced small
2 Tablespoons red pepper, diced small
1 small cucumber, peeled, diced, remove seeds, about 1 cup
3 Tablespoons fresh cilantro, chopped
4 Tablespoons fresh lime juice *(fresh is best)*
Salt and fresh pepper to taste
½ avocado *(optional)*

Combine all ingredients in a bowl. Add salt and pepper to taste. ½ avocado *(optional)* If it is too hot, this will temper the taste. Serves 4-6

Papaya-Mango Salsa

1 papaya, skinned and diced fine
1 mango, skinned and diced fine
1 jalapeno pepper, diced very fine
1 red pepper, diced fine
1 small red onion, diced
1 Tablespoon olive oil
1 teaspoon cumin
Salt and pepper to taste

Combine all ingredients to make salsa. Let stand and refrigerate over night. Can be kept in refrigerator for several weeks.

Papaya-Mango Salsa   ©Connie Hope

Tomatillo Salsa with Red Bell Peppers

¾ cup diced tomatillos, husk removed

¼ cup diced red bell pepper

¼ cup diced red onion

2 Tablespoons orange juice

4 Tablespoons white wine vinegar

2 Tablespoons fresh lime juice

2 Tablespoons fresh lemon juice

1 Tablespoon sugar

½ teaspoon minced seeded jalapeno pepper

Puree ¼ cup tomatillos in processor. Put ½ cup diced tomatillos and ¼ cup pureed into bowl. Mix remaining ingredients in bowl. Cover and refrigerate for 1 hour. Serves 4-6

Tomatillo-Celery Salsa

1 lb fresh tomatillos *(about 10-12 tomatillos)*

4 pieces of celery

1 cup packed fresh cilantro, chopped

6 radishes

1 fresh lemon juice

Remove husk and rinse tomatillos under warm water. Dice about 1/2 of the tomatillos. Puree remaining tomatillos in blender or food processor. Cut and chop celery into ¼ inch pieces. Chop cilantro. Slice radishes and cut into strips. Toss ingredients in a bowl and season with salt and pepper. Add lemon juice. Refrigerate for 1 hour. Serves 4-6

Tomatillo-Celery Salsa   ©Connie Hope

Serve with:

Chips
Fish
Shrimp
Pork Chops
Ham

©Connie Hope

Two Options:
1. ½ red pepper, chopped fine and added for color
2. To kick up the heat a little, use ½ small jalapeno pepper cleaned, seeded, and chopped.

Serve with:

Corn chips
Taco chips
Crackers
Eggs

This is a salsa with the taste of pineapple and the spice of the jalapeno peppers. You may want to try tasting after you add each jalapeno pepper to the mixture. This is just in case it is too hot. You can always add more, but you can't take it away.

Serve with:

Fish
Chicken

Or even as a dessert

This really has a great flavor.

Incredible Edible Salsa

1 can stewed tomatoes (28 oz), sprained juice

3 large jalapenos

Salt to taste

½ teaspoon cumin powder

4 cloves of garlic peeled, chopped

½ teaspoon oregano

¼ cup cilantro leaves

Roast the jalapenos in the oven under the broiler until skins are blackened. Blend jalapenos in only the juice of stewed tomatoes. Add the seasonings and garlic. Add the tomatoes and cilantro leaves to blender and chop. Ready to serve with your favorite taco chips. Keep refrigerated. Serves 4-6

Fresh Pineapple Salsa

2 cups fresh pineapple, chopped in chunks (or canned)
½ cup red bell pepper, chopped

2-4 jalapeno peppers, minced (depending on your taste)

½ medium white onion, chopped

1 Tablespoon rice wine vinegar *(or substitute wine vinegar)*

1 teaspoon sugar

¼ teaspoon salt

Mix first four ingredients in a bowl. In separate bowl mix vinegar, sugar, and salt together. Pour over pineapple mixture. Mix well. Refrigerate before serving. Serves 6-8

Tropical 'Fruitie' Salsa

½ ripe papaya, diced
1 ripe mango, diced

1/6 cantaloupe, diced

2 kiwis, peeled and diced

6-8 medium strawberries, diced

¾ cup watermelon, diced and seeds removed

½ teaspoon sugar

3 Tablespoons water

2-3 Tablespoons fresh cilantro, chopped fine

Salt and pepper to taste

Combine all fruits, stir in cilantro. Serves 6-8

Chutney

Chutney is a strongly spiced condiment of Indian origin. The first Indian chutneys reaching the West appeared as luxury imports in England and France during the late 1600's. These were mostly made as mango chutneys. The Westerners copied these recipes and some of the most popular substitutes were unripened peaches or melons.

Chutneys are made of fruit or vegetables. Chutney is similar to 'salsa' of the Latin American cuisine or 'relish' of the European cuisine. It is typically served as an accompaniment to food, not as a spread. Chutneys are made fresh in small amounts and finished quickly. The spice level can range from mild to hot, and sweet or sour to spicy. The consistency is from a fine or smooth relish to a chunky preserve consistency. A chutney is made with fresh ingredients and might be raw or cooked. Some of the most common chutneys are those made with mangoes, cranberries, pears, peaches, berries, and ground leaves of herbs such as mint, coriander, or cilantro. Fruit chutney consists of chopped fruit, vinegar, spices, sugar, and a significant amount of fresh green chili peppers cooked into a chunky sweet-tart-spicy mix. They bring color and variety to your entrée.

Chutney is my favorite to make and serve in addition to the entree. It adds so much to the main course and there are so many different kinds and different tastes. Sometimes I just can't choose which one to make. That is why I have included so many of my favorites in this cookbook. Soon I will write a cookbook solely with different chutneys.

When you try a few, I know you will find your favorites, too. Then you'll be able to dash into your kitchen to add variety to the tastes on your dinner plate with your favorite chutney in addition... to the entrée.

©Connie Hope

Chutney is spelled chatni in India

A chutney can be served cold or hot with most meals.

Serve with:
Fish
Chicken
Ham

Apple-Date Chutney

2/3 cup chopped red onion

¾ cup chopped peeled tart green apple

¼ cup chopped pitted dates

2 Tablespoons apple juice

1 Tablespoon wine vinegar

4 Tablespoons olive oil

¼ teaspoon curry powder

Heat oil in a skillet, add onion and sauté until soften. Mix in apple, dates, apple juice, and 1 tsp of curry powder. Cook for 4-5 minutes add vinegar and simmer few minutes. Can be refrigerated for several weeks. Makes 3-4 half pints

Apple-Date Chutney   ©Connie Hope

Serve with:

Brie
Cream Cheese Square

Ham
Pork Chop

Apricot-Rosemary Chutney

12 oz dried apricots, chopped (between 14 and 16 apricots)

1 large red onion, chopped fine

1 cup water

2/3 cup cider vinegar

2/3 cup packed golden brown sugar

¾ cup dried tart cherries (canned or fresh)

½ Tablespoon chopped fresh rosemary

1 large garlic clove, finely chopped

1 teaspoon grated lemon peel

½ teaspoon salt

1/8 teaspoon cayenne pepper

½ cup blanched, slivered almonds, toasted

Combine all ingredients in a medium sauce pan. Heat over medium heat for 10 minutes. Can be refrigerated for several weeks. Makes 3-plus half pints

Apple-Ginger Chutney

4 Granny Smith apples, cored, peeled, and chopped

1 cup golden raisins

2 cups minced onions—can use red onions

1 ½ cups brown sugar firmly packed

1 ½ cups cider vinegar

¼ cup minced peeled fresh ginger root

1 red bell pepper, minced very fine

¾ teaspoon dry mustard

¾ teaspoon salt

½ teaspoon dried hot red pepper flakes or cayenne pepper —
or 1 teaspoon red hot sauce *(You can use Gloria's West Indies Pepper Sauce listed in index.)*

In a large sauce pan combine all ingredients. Bring mixture to a boil, stirring continually. Cook over moderate heat for 40 minutes or until thickened. Can be refrigerated for several weeks. Makes 4-6 half pint jars.

Apple-Green Tomato Chutney

1 seeded chopped lemon

1 skinned chopped clove garlic

2 ½ cups firm peeled chopped apples

2 ½ cups green tomatoes *

2 ¼ cups brown sugar

1 ½ cups seeded raisins

3 oz. chopped crystallized ginger or ¼ cup fresh ginger root

1 ½ teaspoons salt

¼ teaspoon cayenne

2 cups cider vinegar

2 chopped red peppers, seeds and membrane removed

Combine all ingredients in a large pot. Simmer for a least 2 hours or until thickened. Can be refrigerated for several weeks. Makes 6-7 half pints.

©Connie Hope

Serve with :

This chutney is excellent with ham.

It also complements pork chops or a pork roast.

I usually make this chutney in the fall when the tomatoes are on the vine, but are green with little chance that they will ripen before the cold weather.

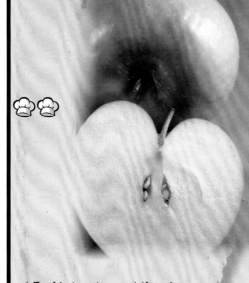

* To skin tomatoes, put them in boiling water for 1 minute longer if they are large tomatoes 1½ minutes then put them immediately in iced cold water. The skins will come off easily.

Serve with:
Ham
Pork
Hamburgers
Hot Dogs

©Connie Hope

Berry Chutney *(Use fresh blueberries or elderberries)*

1 lb Granny Smith apples
1 lb berries, washed
½ cup dried currants or raisins
1 cup chopped fine white onion
½ teaspoon ground ginger
1 teaspoon salt
1 cup vinegar (malt is my favorite, but any is good)
1 ½ cups of brown sugar
½ teaspoon cinnamon, nutmeg, and red pepper flakes

Peel and chop apples. Mix berries, raisins, onions, and apples in a large saucepan. Stir in the spices, salt, and ½ cup vinegar. Cook slowly and stir for 1 hour until berries are soft. Remove from the heat and gently stir in the sugar. Add the remaining ½ cup vinegar. When the sugar has completely dissolved, return the sauce pan to the heat and bring to a boil. Boil for 20-30 minutes stirring continually so it does not stick. Mixture should have thickened. Refrigerate for 2 weeks. Makes 4-6 half pints.

Cherry Chutney

2 cups pitted cherries
½ cup raisins
1 teaspoon cinnamon
½ cup brown sugar
¼ teaspoon clove
¾ cup honey
¾ cup pecans chopped—optional

Combine all ingredients except the pecans. Simmer slowly for 1- 1 ½ hours. Stir often. At the last 5 minutes add the pecans. Can be refrigerated for a week. Makes 3-5 half pint jars.

Cranberry Chutney

4 cups cranberries, fresh or frozen

¾ cup brown sugar

½ cup raisins

½ cup chopped celery

½ cup chopped apples

½ cup chopped pears

½ cup water

¼ cup chopped walnuts-coarse

2 Tablespoons minced candied ginger

2 Tablespoons lemon juice

¼ teaspoon ground cloves

1 teaspoon onion salt

Bring all ingredients to a boil. Stir constantly. Simmer for 15 minutes. Keep in refrigerator up to 2 weeks. Makes 4-6 half pints

If you would like an additional variation, add ½ cup whiskey to the mix.

Serve with:
Turkey
Ham
Pork
Tofu Turkey

Cranberry-Orange Chutney

3 cups cranberries, fresh or frozen

1 cup chopped onions

1 cup raisins

1 cup currants

1 cup vinegar, cider is best

¾ cup sugar

¾ cup brown sugar packed

1 Tablespoon grated orange zest (the rind)

½ cup orange juice

1 teaspoon salt

1 teaspoon cinnamon

1 teaspoon ginger

1 teaspoon clove, ground

In a saucepan, stir cranberries, onions, raisins, currants, vinegar, two sugars, orange zest, and juice. salt, cinnamon, ginger, and cloves. Bring to a boil. Reduce heat and simmer. Stir continually for 20 minutes. Mixture will thicken. Can refrigerate for at least a week. Makes 3-5 half pints

This one has a nice taste of orange.

Variations:
Eliminate the grated orange and orange juice.

Add ½ cup peeled, diced apples.
Or
Add 16 dried apricots, halved, then quartered

Serve with:
Turkey
Ham
Pork
Tofu Turkey

Cranberry-Apricot Chutney

1 ½ cups fresh cranberries

16 dried apricots, halved then quartered

¾ cup brown sugar

1/3 cup currants or raisins

2 Tablespoons fresh ginger minced

2 Tablespoons cranberry cocktail juice

¾ teaspoon ground cumin

¼ teaspoon cayenne pepper

Combine all ingredients in a heavy sauce pan and cook at medium heat to dissolve sugar. Bring to a boil for 3 minutes until cranberries pop. Stir. Let cool and can be refrigerated for up to 2 weeks. Makes 3-4 half pints

Cranberry-Apricot Chutney   ©Connie Hope

Cranberry-Apple Chutney

16 oz can of whole berry cranberry sauce, canned

½ cup raisins

½ cup peeled, diced apple

¼ cup + 2 Tablespoons sugar

¼ cup + 2 Tablespoons vinegar

1/8 teaspoon allspice

1/8 teaspoon ginger

1/8 teaspoon cinnamon

Dash ground cloves

Combine all ingredients in a medium saucepan. Cook on medium heat for about 20-30 minutes or until apples are tender. Stir occasionally. Sauce should have thickened slightly. Refrigerate for two weeks. Makes 3-4 plus half pints.

©Connie Hope

Creamy Mint-Cilantro Chutney

1/3 cup sliced almonds

¾ cup fresh mint leaves, chopped and packed

¾ cup fresh cilantro, chopped and packed

3 Tablespoons sour cream

2 teaspoons honey

½ teaspoon minced garlic

Preheat oven to 325 F. Toast almonds in one layer on a baking sheet until golden brown, about 10 minutes, and then cool. Finely grind almonds in a food processor. Add remaining ingredients. Salt and pepper to taste, Blend until smooth. Can be refrigerated for a week. Makes 2 half pints

Mint-Pineapple Chutney

1 ½ cups fresh mint leaves, packed, rinsed, towel dried, and chopped fine
(You can chop in a food processor or by hand)
1 medium pineapple, cored, peeled, and diced *(or 20 oz can*
and 10 oz can, drained)

¼ cup sugar

½ cup Bermuda onion (purple onion)

1/8 teaspoon of salt (or to taste)

Combine fresh mint and pineapple in a large bowl. Add the onion, sugar, and salt. Stir until mixture has become a homogeneous mix. Cover the bowl and allow to stand for at least 2 hours before using. Can be refrigerated for one week. Makes 4 half pints

Serve with:

Chicken
Beef
Fish

Serve with:
Grilled fish
Ham
Lamb

©Connie Hope

Serve with:

Serve with:
Fish: Baked or broiled
Ham
Pork

Fruit and Nut Chutney

2 cups dried apricots

2 inches fresh ginger, peeled/cut into medium sized pieces

1-2 cloves of garlic, peeled and diced

¼ cup of red wine vinegar

2 ⅛ cups of brown sugar

½ teaspoon of cayenne pepper

¾ cup of golden raisins

½ cup almonds (optional)**, sliced**

½ cup currants

½ teaspoon salt

Rinse dried apricots, cut into small chunks. Soak apricots and almonds in 4 cups hot water for 1 ½ hrs. Make a paste in food processor using ½ vinegar, ginger, and garlic. Then add remaining vinegar and pour into a stainless steel sauce pan. Add to the pot the apricots and nuts and the water they have soaked in. Then add the sugar and cayenne. Bring to a boil, then simmer for half an hour. Continually stir and add the raisins and currants. Continue to simmer for a half hour and add salt. Can be store in refrigerator for several weeks. Makes about 3 half pints.

Serve with:

Pork
Ham

Can be used over ice cream,
pound cake, or pudding

Hot 'Fruitie" Chutney

4 Tablespoons butter

6 teaspoon brown sugar

2 ½ cups pineapple chunks, drain and save juice

Small amount of pineapple juice

4 bananas.

In a heavy skillet melt butter. Peel bananas and cut into slices. Add sugar, pineapples, and small amount of pineapple juice. Cook slowly until fruit is hot and sauce is bubbling. Best to serve the same day. Makes 3-4 half pints

Mango Chutney

2 fresh mangos—firm

1 Tablespoon lemon juice (fresh is best)

3 Tablespoons red onion (Bermuda onion) minced

1 jalapeno pepper, minced (I prefer removing the seeds
    which are very hot.)

1 Tablespoon ginger root minced

Dash of nutmeg and cinnamon

¼ to ½ cup cilantro, chopped coarsely

Peel mango, remove the meat, cut in chucks *(see appendix on 'How to Cut a Mango')* Put all ingredients (holding aside the cilantro and mango) in a food processor and pulse several times. Put mixture including the mango in a pot and simmer for 15 minutes on low heat. Add the cilantro and mix. Can be refrigerated for several days. Makes 3-4 half pints

Lime-Mango Chutney

4 cups sliced mango

1 onion, chopped coarsely

6 limes, juiced

1 cup sugar (option: substitute brown sugar)

1 cup raisins

1 clove of garlic or ¼ teaspoon minced garlic

½ cup sliced almonds

½ to 1 teaspoon cayenne

1 Tablespoon ginger, chopped

1 Tablespoon mustard seeds

Add all ingredients in a large pot.
Cook slowly for 40 minutes. Fruit should be soft, but not mushy.
Can be kept in refrigerator for several days. Makes about 4 half pints

©Connie Hope

Mango goes well with most fish and meats.
It is one of my favorites with grouper.

White fish
All fish
Pork Chops
Tofu

Remember to use rubber gloves with the peppers.

This is a really good tangy chutney.

Serve with:
Fish
Ham
Pork
Baked tofu

This is lemony chutney with a nice sweetness. It blends with the hot chili powder, the grated ginger, and the licorice taste of anise.

This compliments a salad, barbecued chicken, or just plain hamburgers

Serve with:
Ham
Pork Chops
Shrimp
Fish

Pineapple-Anise Chutney

1 large pineapple, under ripe so it is firm and stays together when cut. Peel, core, and chunk pineapple or 1 large can

3 lemons juiced

Zest of 1 lemon (this is the grating of the skin of a lemon).

2 Tablespoons fresh grated ginger

1 cup apple cider vinegar

1 large white onion chopped fine in the food processor

½ cup golden raisins (or currants)

1 teaspoon of chili powder

1 teaspoon anise

½ teaspoon curry powder

1 cup sugar

½ teaspoon salt

Bring the vinegar and sugar to a boil in a deep saucepan. Add all other listed ingredients and bring back to a boil. Remove from the heat source and let stand for at least 30-35 minutes. Place pan back on heat and boil gently for 30 minutes. Make sure you stir continually because it could stick. Refrigerate for up to 1 week. Makes 3-4 + half pints

Pineapple Chutney

1 20 oz can pineapple chunks

½ cup raisins

½ onion, chopped

1/3 cup brown sugar, packed

½ cup cider vinegar

½ teaspoon ginger, ground

¼ teaspoon curry powder

¼ teaspoon cloves, ground

dash cayenne

salt

Combine all ingredients in a sauce pan.
Bring to a boil, then reduce heat and simmer for one hour, uncovered, stir occasionally Let cool. Refrigerator for up to 1 week. Makes 3-4 half pints

Pumpkin Chunk Chutney

4 cups chunked pumpkin

2 cups sugar

1 lemon, sliced very thin

Juice of ½ orange

Grated rind of ½ orange

4 Tablespoons finely diced crystallized ginger

Wash pumpkin and cut off outside thick skin. Cut inside of pumpkin into small chunks, removing all seeds. Put the seeds aside in another container. (See below) Combine pumpkin chunks with sugar, orange rind, orange juice, lemon, (cut thin) and ginger. Using a medium size heavy saucepan, stir ingredients over moderate heat until mixture boils. Lower heat to cook slowly for 15 minutes (or until the pumpkin chunks are translucent.) Cool. Can store in refrigerator 1 week. Makes 3-5 half pints

Pumpkin Seeds

1. After you have chunked the pumpkin, take the seeds from the pumpkin that you put aside.

2. Separate the pulp from the seeds and discard the pulp.

3. Wash the seeds in warm water using a strainer.

4. Spread seeds out on a cookie sheet.

5. Sprinkle with salt to your taste.

6. Bake at 350 degrees for 20 minutes.

7. Check at five minute intervals, stirring, and add a little more salt to taste.

8. Allow to cool and eat.

9. You can also sprinkle with cheesy seasoning or Cajun seasonings mix instead of salt.

©Connie Hope

The fall is the best time to make this chutney because pumpkins are easy to find. This is really yummy.

Water bathing the recipe will allow you to have a stock for several months.

Serve with: :

Ham
Turkey
Tofu

Pumpkin Note:

1. Is a pumpkin a squash?
2. Do pumpkins contain potassium and Vitamin A?
3. Are pumpkin flowers edible?

1. Yes
2. Yes
3. Yes

You will not be able to stop eating these seeds! *Yum*.

* To roast mustard seeds, pour a small amount of oil in a fry pan, add mustard seeds in oil and let sizzle for 10-15 seconds. Then put into a small bowl and set aside.

This is good for making a 'quick' chutney.

Serve with:

Ham
Turkey
Pasta
Tofu

©Connie Hope

Tomato-Onion Chutney

2½ cups chopped onions (I like to use red onion)

1 teaspoon mustard seeds, roasted*

3 ½ Tablespoons butter or margarine

14 oz can of tomatoes, drained. Make sure they are diced in smaller pieces.
(Fresh tomatoes can be used, but they will need to be skinned, drained, and diced)

2 Tablespoons red wine vinegar or malt vinegar

2 Tablespoons minced fresh parsley leaves (Fresh is always better, or use dried, but use less)

1 Tablespoon sugar

1/8 teaspoon ground allspice

In a heavy skillet, cook onions in butter over a medium heat. Cook until the mixture of onions has turned golden. Add the tomatoes, the vinegar, the sugar, the allspice, and roasted mustard seeds . Cook mixture, stirring with a wooden spoon until the chutney has thickened. Add the parsley and salt and pepper to taste. Can be refrigerated up to 1 week.

Quick Tomato and Red Onion Chutney

No cooking needed

½ cup chopped red onion

½ cup chopped seeded plum tomatoes

½ cup chopped fresh mint

1 Tablespoon fresh lime juice

¼ teaspoon cayenne pepper

Combine all ingredients in medium mixing bowl. Salt and pepper to taste. Let stand for several hours stirring occasionally. Makes about 2 half pints. Refrigerate for up to 1 week.

Relish and Pickles

The dictionary defines a relish as a cooked, pickled and/or chopped vegetable or fruit that is used as a condiment. (A condiment is an aromatic mixture, such as pickles, chutney, and some sauces and relishes, that accompanies food.). Typically, a relish is pickled using vinegar (see next page on types of vinegar). In the United States the most common type of relish is made from finely chopped sweet pickles and served with hamburgers or hot dogs. Think about it. What would that hot dog or hamburger be like without catsup and relish? Not really that good. This is the Indian relish or the sweet pickle relish we typically serve. Whipping up some of this well-known condiment at home is quick, easy, and fun. Not to mention that it will taste much better than the supermarket brands. And you did it yourself.

Some argue that a relish is made with vegetables, while chutney is made with fruit. However, both chutney and relishes can be sweet or savory or spicy. Although I would say that the relish is usually crunchier and uses less sugar than the chutney. And the chutney has a chunky, 'spreadable' consistency with more sugar. So the choice is yours. These condiments usually go a long way since the flavor is concentrated and adds a zing to a dish. They are complementing each other.

When the word "pickle" is used, most of us envision the small cucumber as a pickle, but in food processing or canning, the term "pickle" or "pickling" is a process rather than an object. To pickle is either a salt brine solution or a vinegar solution. In reality to pickle you can use the cucumber, fruit, vegetables, or even meats.

Pickled cucumbers are a common feature in vegetable relishes, although other veggies may be pickled in a relish for more flavor and added texture. Good examples are carrots, onions, peppers, eggplant, cabbage, and cauliflower. Generally, vegetable relishes may be made savory, tart, sweet, or spicy, depending on the taste of the cook. Vegetable relishes often go well with meats; examples are sausage or roasts. The word 'pickles' and 'relishes' are similar and sometimes interchangeable .

I think of a relish as pickles and chutney as fruit with flavors and spices.

They are really interchangeable.

Mango Salsa variation pg 70

Cucumber Relish pg 94

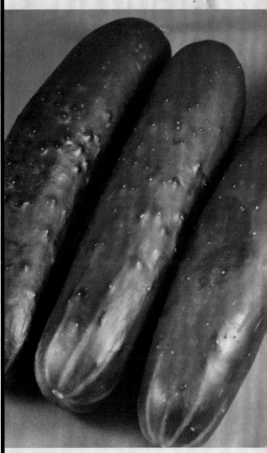

©Connie Hope

Vinegar 101

Dictionaries defines vinegar as "a sour-tasting, highly acidic (acetic acid) liquid made from the oxidation of alcohol, cider, beer, fermented fruit juice, or nearly any other liquid containing alcohol, which is used as a condiment or a preservative."

The airborne bacteria called acetobacter aceti converts the alcohol into acetic acid. Ancient civilization used vinegar as a condiment, a preservative, a medicine, and as a detergent, just as we do today.

The earlier method of making vinegar was to leave wine or beer in a barrel with several large holes that would allow the oxygen in, then wait for it to sour. In fact, the French word 'vinaigre' literally means 'sour wine." The French developed a method of making vinegar by leaving wine in wooden casks for two to six months and it would slowly turn to vinegar. It would be filtered and put into another cask and left again to mature. This might take another few months or a year. This became known as the 'Orleans method." A good wine would be used to produce good vinegar.

In the mid 19th century, Louis Pasteur published scientific research on vinegar. It was this research that was used to create the commercial method of making vinegar. In the commercial method, wine is slowly poured over wood chips in vats. It is this slow movement of the wine over the wood chips that oxidizes the alcohol in the wine and turns it into acetic acid. This technique decreased the average production time from months or years to days. The end result is the tart liquid that we call vinegar.

On the tartness scale of vinegar:

- Distilled white vinegars are the strongest and most astringent
- Wine vinegars are second
- Cider or malt vinegars are in the middle
- Rice wine vinegars are milder
- Balsamic vinegars are most mellow

Let's take a quick look at some of the different types of vinegar.

Cultures around the world have used vinegar in preparing food. Some examples are as part of a marinade, sauce, salsa, mustard, relish, chutney, jelly, and jams.

There are many different types of vinegar and you will find the one or two you enjoy when creating food.

©Connie Hope

Distilled Vinegar

Distilled vinegar is colorless, very strong to the taste, and made from distilled alcohol. It is used in pickling, canning and as a household disinfectant more than culinary cooking. It has a flavor that is course and harsh. It is great for cleaning nonporous surfaces such as glass and coffee pots. It costs the least of all vinegars to make.

Wine Vinegars

As wines come in red and white, so does vinegar. The quality of vinegar is determined by the quality of the wine. Red wine vinegars are aged longer than the white wine vinegars. Red wine vinegar has a more roundness of flavor, while white wine vinegar is used more for light colored sauces and other dishes. Red wine can be used for medical as well as culinary purposes.

Champagne Vinegar-
variation of wine vinegar

This vinegar is much more expensive to make than it is to buy. It is a pale golden color and is clear and bright. It adds a great taste to a recipe. It has a more refined taste, which can be used in sauces, fine salads, and mignonette sauces for oysters.

Sherry Vinegar-
variation of wine vinegar

Sherry vinegars are made from blends of wines, just like the sherry. The taste is smooth and mellow and can be a more expensive vinegar. The wine is left to mature in aged oak casts for a long time. Many gourmet recipes use sherry vinegar.

Apple Cider Vinegar

This type of vinegar is made from apple mash or apple cider. The flavor has a hint of apple, a tart fruity taste, and is honey colored. It is used as a condiment such as salad dressing when diluted and for pickling fruit and making chutneys. It is a good type of vinegar to use for cooking purposes and for health. It does not need to be refrigerated when open and has a shelf life of many years.

There are flavored vinegars, herbed vinegars, fruit vinegars, cane vinegars, and names of the wine vinegars. Examples are Zinfandel, Pinot, Merlot, or Chardonnay vinegars.

©Connie Hope

Malt Vinegar

The English have used malt vinegar for hundreds of years. It has a strong, distinct malt flavor. They are famous for putting malt vinegar on their fish and chips. I know I like it that way.

Malt vinegar is made from a beer-like brew using malted barley in a two-part process. It is left to age in casks, much the same as wine vinegar.

Rice Vinegar

It is made from the fermented rice or rice wine. The origin is from China and Japan. It is mild vinegar with a color range from pale yellow for white rice vinegar to a darker color for the black rice vinegar. There are several types of rice vinegar: white rice vinegar, black rice vinegar and red rice vinegar. The white rice vinegar has a mild and soft flavor similar to regular vinegar. Red rice vinegar is darker in color and has a combination of tart and sweet taste. The black rice vinegar has a deep, almost smoky flavor.

©Connie Hope

Balsamic Vinegar

It is dark brown, almost purple color, with a complex flavor. The longer it is aged the sweeter and thicker it becomes.

According to my research, this vinegar originated in a town in northern Italy called Modena more than six hundred years ago. It was made from the juice of sweet white grapes called Trebbiano grapes, which were boiled down to a thick syrup. It went through two or three fermentation processes and then filtered into wooden casks and left to mature for many years. It was the combination of wood, wine, and time that make this Italian balsamic vinegar rare and expensive.

Today, it is made commercially with a process that has somewhat the same characteristics of the original process, but does not take the same amount of time or encompass the Trebbiano grapes.

Gobble-up Pickles

1 quart cucumbers

1 cup sugar

1 cup cider vinegar

1 teaspoon salt

1 teaspoon dry mustard

1 teaspoon mixed pickling spices

Dash of turmeric for color

Peel and cut cucumber in half lengthwise and remove seeds. Cut cucumber in chunks. Mix ingredients together and cook until tender. Add turmeric for color. Put in sterilized jar and water bath for 30 minutes. Makes 3-4 pints

Cauliflower Pickles

2 medium heads cauliflower

2 cups tiny white onions

¾ cup salt

Ice cubes

1 ¼ cup sugar

2 teaspoons turmeric

2 Tablespoons mustard seeds

1 Tablespoon celery seed

1 hot red pepper-chopped (optional)

Divide cauliflower into flowerets. Remove outside skin on onions. Add salt to vegetables and mix with ice cubes. Cover with more ice cubes and let stand at least 3 hours. Drain, but save liquid. Mix remaining ingredients in large pot. Bring to a boil and stir to dissolve sugar. Add cauliflower and onions. Cook 10 minutes or until tender. Reheat liquid. Put cauliflower in sterilized jars and add reheated liquid. Water bath for 30 minutes. Makes 3-4 pints

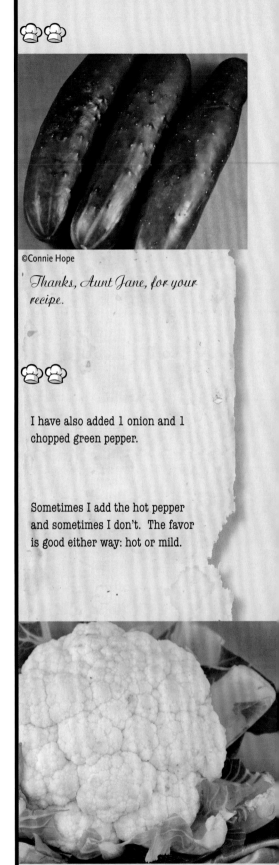

©Connie Hope

Thanks, Aunt Jane, for your recipe.

I have also added 1 onion and 1 chopped green pepper.

Sometimes I add the hot pepper and sometimes I don't. The favor is good either way: hot or mild.

©Connie Hope

An Italian style dish to serve with
any meat

Serve with:
Beef
Hamburgers
Chicken

*I use jalapeno or serrano peppers
cut very fine. I am sure if you like
things 'hot,' you could use a habanera
pepper.

If you put the pint jar on its side and
lay the okra inside, it works well. You
can really stuff a lot of okra into it. I
try to put a clove of garlic and celery
leaves in each jar.

I have also cut the recipe in half to
make only 3+ pints.

They are good with hamburgers and
hot dogs.

I use these even for appetizers. They
are excellent!
Yummy.

Pickled Mushrooms

2 pounds of small mushrooms (I use the button ones)

1 cup water

1 ½ cups Italian salad dressing- your favorite

1 Tablespoon mixed pickling spices

Place small mushrooms in a steamer and steam for about 8- 10 minutes or
until mushrooms are tender. Save liquid and let cool. Mix 1 ½ cups Italian
salad dressing with pickling spices and put into either ½ pint or pint sterilized jars. Add mushrooms and top with the saved liquid. Refrigerate and
store for 3 days before using.

Okra Pickles

2 pounds small okra pods

2 cups white distilled vinegar

2 cups water

1/3 cup salt

3 small hot peppers, ✻ chopped finely (optional)

4-6 garlic cloves (use as many as you like)

1- 1 ½ teaspoons dill weed

Celery leaves, chopped

Clean and wash the okra pods. Trim if needed. Pack okra firmly in sterilized
jars-either ½ pint or pint jars. Put remaining ingredients in a pot. Bring to a
boil then, pour over the okra in the jar and seal. Water bath for 15 minutes.
Makes 5-7 pints Let stand for several weeks before using.

©Connie Hope

Chow-Chow Relish

3 cups cauliflower-chopped
2 teaspoons dry mustard
1 small head of cabbage-chopped
1 teaspoon turmeric
2 cups onions-chopped
½ teaspoon ground ginger
2 cups green tomatoes (4 medium)
2 teaspoons celery seed
2 cups sweet green peppers-chopped
1 teaspoon mustard seed
1 cup sweet red pepper-chopped
3 Tablespoons salt
2 ½ cups cider vinegar
1 ½ cups sugar

©Connie Hope

Mix chopped vegetables and cover with salt. Allow to stand 4-6 hours in a cool place. Drain. Combine vinegar, sugar, and spices. Simmer 10-15 minutes. Add vegetables and simmer 10 minutes. Bring to a boil. Put in sterilized jars. Make sure that the rim is cleaned, lid and ring on. Water bath for 30 minutes. Makes about 4-5 pints.

Beet Relish

2-3 medium size beets
2 cups chopped cabbage
¼ teaspoon pepper
½ teaspoon red pepper
½ teaspoon salt
1 cup chopped celery
¾ cup sugar
1 cup vinegar (use your favorite type)
½ cup water

Boil the beets.
Let cool for a few minutes, then remove outside skin.* Chop. Mix all ingredients together and bring to a boil. Turn to medium heat for 5 minutes. Put in sterilized jar and water bath for 30 minutes. Makes 3-4 half pints

There are as many recipes for Chow-Chow as there are for chocolate chip cookies. Each has a little different ingredient.

Finding the recipe you enjoy best can be a challenge, but fun in the experiments.

This is my favorite.

This is great with beef, corn beef, or pork chops

*Removing the skin of a beet:
If you pick it up in your hands and pull, the skins will slide right off.

©Connie Hope

There are many recipes for pic-
calilli. This is my favorite and I
find this has the best flavor.

Cranberry-Jalapeno Relish

1 bag (12 oz) fresh cranberries

1 lime, cleaned

¾ cup sugar

2-3 jalapeno peppers, seeded and minced (use gloves)

¼ cup chopped fresh cilantro

Food process cranberries until coarsely chopped. Put into bowl. Cut lime with peel into small chucks. Process until finely diced. Add to cranberries along with sugar and minced jalapeno. *(Start with 2 jalapeno peppers and taste if you need it hotter, if so add another half or whole pepper.)* Mix in cilantro. Refrigerate relish for several hours before serving. The standing allows flavors to blend. Serve chilled. Serves 3-4

Piccalilli

4 cups cabbage, chopped

4 cups green tomatoes, chopped

2 sweet red peppers, chopped

2 sweet green peppers, chopped

2 large yellow onions, chopped

½ cup salt

1 ½ cups vinegar

1 ½ cups water

2 cups firmly packed brown sugar

1 teaspoon dry mustard

1 teaspoon turmeric

1 teaspoon celery seed

Chop the cabbage, tomatoes, peppers, and onion. Mix chopped vegetables with salt and allow to set overnight in the refrigerator. Let drain and press to remove all liquids. Boil vinegar, water, sugar, and spices for about 5-6 minutes. Add chopped vegetables. Bring to a boil and continue for 1 minute. Put in sterilized jars, make sure rim is clean. Put lid and ring on and water bath for 30 minutes. Makes 6 pints or about 12 ½ pint jars.

Cranberry-Orange Relish

2 large navel oranges, skin cleaned

4 cups fresh cranberries

1 ½ cups sugar

Cut and quarter oranges, leaving skins on but removing membranes and seeds. Clean and chop cranberries, coarsely (I put them in a food processor and pulse it). Mix orange and cranberries together and add sugar. Mix well and refrigerate. This will keep at least a week, so you can prepare it ahead. Makes about 4-5 pints.

Mango Relish

1 mango, diced

2 Tablespoons lime juice (I usually add more)

2 Tablespoons fresh cilantro, chopped

1 clove garlic or ¼ teaspoon minced garlic

2 Tablespoons fresh parsley, chopped

Fresh ground pepper and salt to taste

Combine mango, lime juice, and spices. Refrigerate until needed. Serves 4-6

Corn Relish

2 cups sweet corn (fresh or canned)

1 cup cherry tomatoes, chopped

½ cup purple onion, very finely chopped

2-3 teaspoons red wine vinegar

3 teaspoons virgin olive oil

2 Tablespoons fresh basil chopped (I add more)

Salt and fresh pepper to taste

Put the olive oil, vinegar, salt and pepper in a large bowl. Whisk for a few minutes to combine. Add the remaining ingredients. Cover and chill before serving.

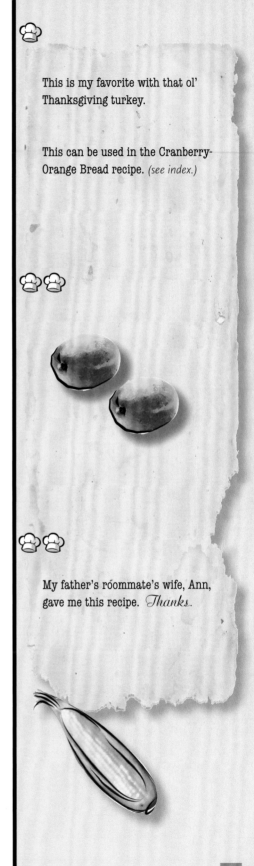

This is my favorite with that ol' Thanksgiving turkey.

This can be used in the Cranberry-Orange Bread recipe. *(see index.)*

My father's roommate's wife, Ann, gave me this recipe. *Thanks.*

This is great with hot dogs and hamburgers.

I use it with pork chops and ham slices.

Excellent with all fish,
(I love it with salmon)
as well as hamburgers,
and hot dogs too.

Corn Relish *(variation)*

5 cups corn (either frozen or canned)
½ cup chopped green peppers
½ cup chopped sweet red peppers
½ cup chopped onion (I like to use a purple onion for color)
½ cup chopped celery
1 Tablespoon salt
¾ cup sugar
1 Tablespoon mustard seed
¼ teaspoon turmeric
½ teaspoon celery seed
1 ¼ cups white vinegar
1 cup water

Combine all ingredients and bring to a boil. Boil for about 15 minutes. Put in sterilized jars ½ pint or pint jars. Make sure rim is clean, put on lid and ring on. Water bath for 30 minutes. Makes 6-7 half pints

Cucumber Relish

2 cups chopped cucumber, peeled
½ cup chopped red bell pepper
½ cup chopped onion
2 Tablespoons chopped fresh mint
1 Tablespoon capers
1 Tablespoon cider vinegar
¼ teaspoon salt

Combine all ingredients together.
Mix thoroughly and refrigerate for several hours.

©Connie Hope

Watermelon Pickles

3 pounds of watermelon rind
1 quart water
3 Tablespoons of salt

Syrup

4 cups sugar

2 cups water

2 cups vinegar

1 lemon, sliced thin

2 sticks of cinnamon

2 Tablespoons whole cloves

2 Tablespoons allspice

Thoroughly wash watermelon rind. This is the white area of the watermelon. Remove the skin. Cut into small pieces. Soak overnight in a solution made by adding 3 Tablespoons of salt to 1 quart of water. In the morning, remove the watermelon rind and drain. Cook until tender in fresh water. Add the rind to the hot syrup (see below) and bring to a rapid boil for several minutes. Pour into sterilized jars, clean rims, and put on lids and rings. Water bath for 30 minutes. Makes 5-6 pints

Syrup
Make a syrup by cooking the sugar, water, and vinegar together in a large pot. Tie the lemon and spices in a cheese cloth bag and let the bag stay in the syrup with the watermelon rind.

Pickled Eggs

4 cups white vinegar

½ cup sugar

2 Tablespoons pickling spices

2 teaspoon salt

2 bay leaves

1 cup beet juice

2 dozen hard boiled eggs

Bring this mix to a boil. Let cool, then put hard boiled eggs in a container with mixture and store in refrigerator for several weeks.

My Aunt Jane loved to make pickles of all kinds. This was her favorite recipe. She loved to watch me eat and enjoy them.

Beet Juice
Put 3-4 beets in 2 cups water and slowly boil until tender. Save liquid for the pickled eggs.

©Connie Hope

Connie's Cooking Tips:

- Always use fresh, firm vegetables and fruit. Discard if they become soft.

- Vinegar can be used to clean windows. It can also be used to clean your eye glasses.

- When you are learning to cook or experimenting with new recipes, choose recipes that are not complicated. Unusual ingredients or difficult steps can be overwhelming. Start out simple, then progress.

- Cabbages—Look for heads that are heavier than expected and have crisp leaves.

- If your recipe only calls for 1/2 onion, use the other side from the root. The root section will keep longer.

- When a recipe calls for an onion, what type do you use?

  1. Making a salad, use white onions for flavor, red onions and green onions for appearance.

  2. If your recipe seems to need a sweeter onion, use Vidalia onions or super sweet onions.

  3. Recipes that say 'onion' usually mean the yellow onion, which are the most common.

  4. Organic onions have a stronger flavor then regular grown onions.

©Connie Hope

©Connie Hope

Desserts and Breads

I have never been much for really sweet things, but sometimes after a nice dinner there is nothing like a little taste of indulgence. Here are a few of my favorite recipes for those times you need a 'sweet.' Most of these recipes I have had for many years. Some are from friends and some are from relatives. All are great.

Italian Cheese Cake with Crust

(below)

3 cups ricotta cheese, not skim

2 8 oz cream cheese, softened

1 16 oz sour cream

6 eggs, beaten

1 ½ cups sugar

1 Tablespoon lemon juice (fresh is best)

1 Tablespoon vanilla extract

7-8 Tablespoons of flour

Crust (see below)

Combine all ingredients and mix until smooth. Put into a greased springform pan. Bake at 350 degrees for one hour. Turn oven off and allow the cheese cake to remain in oven for one more hour. After it has been in oven for an hour, remove outside pan. When you serve, you can use a fruit sauce.

Crust *(use with the cheese cake)*

1 ½ cups graham cracker crumbs

6 Tablespoons of melted butter or margarine

3 Tablespoon sugar

Preheat oven to 350 degrees. Combine crumbs, butter, and sugar. Press crumbs onto bottom and up about 1 inch on side of pan. Bake for 10-12 minutes until set. Remove from oven and let cool before you put the cheese cake mix in the pan.

©Connie Hope

This is a creamy and 'cheesie' cheese cake.

My son loves cheese cake and I have made this for him several times.

Here's how flexible this crust recipe is. I was making this at a friend's house for my son and their oven broke. I could not bake the crust. So I put it in the freezer for 20 minutes and then added cheese mix. I had to go to a neighbor's house to cook the cheese cake, but the crust came out great. Just use your imagination.

Don't be upset if the edges brown a little or there is a slight incline in a section of the cake. Make sure the oven door is closed when it is cooling. This will prevent some 'falling' of the cheese cake.

Any of the sauces can be used on this cheese cake.

©Connie Hope

I made this for my daughter's birthday. It is excellent and if you don't tell anyone, Shh, no one will guess it is vegan. 'I'll never tell!'

This sauce can be used on any cheesecake, pudding, pound cake, or ice cream.

Vegan Cheesecake

1 ½ cups graham cracker crumbs

1/3 cup vegan margarine, melted

2 Tablespoons sugar

12 oz silken tofu

3 containers of vegan cream cheese

¼ cup pineapple juice

6 Tablespoons vegan margarine

1 Tablespoon lemon juice (fresh is best)

1 Tablespoon vanilla extract

2/3 cup sugar

1 heaping Tablespoon egg replacer

Raspberry Sauce (optional)

Mix first three ingredients together. Press into springform pan or round cake pan. Bake 350 degrees for 10 minutes. Put the remaining ingredients in a blender. Blend until silky and smooth. Pour into crust. Bake for 35-45 minutes. Turn off the oven and leave in for another 15 minutes. Edges should be a golden brown. Let cool for 4-5 hours before serving. Drizzle raspberry sauce (optional)

Raspberry Sauce

6 oz frozen raspberries (use fresh if they are in season)
¼ cup sugar

Heat ingredients until sugar is dissolved. Stir continually. Cover and let simmer low until raspberries are thawed. Use a hand mixer and mix the sauce until smooth. Drizzle on cheesecake. Serve either hot or cold on cheesecake.

©Connie Hope

More Sauces for Cheesecake

Blueberry Sauce

6-8 oz package of frozen blueberries
¼ cup sugar

Combine ingredients and heat covered slowly to defrost berries. Put in food processor and mix for 2-3 minutes until smooth. You can put through a sieve if you want it smoother.

Strawberry Sauce

1 pint fresh strawberries, cleaned and cut
¼ cup sugar—if the strawberries are sweet, you may
want to decrease sugar.
1 teaspoon vanilla extract

Combine in a pot and heat on medium until the berries are soft and falling apart. If you choose, you can food process the berries. I prefer them chunky.

Lemon Sauce

¼ cup lemon juice (either fresh or bottled)
1/3 cup sugar
2 teaspoons cornstarch for thickener
½ cup water
1 egg yolk
1 Tablespoon butter
Yellow food coloring

Combine sugar and cornstarch in a pot. Add water, lemon juice, and egg yolk. Heat over medium heat and stir until mixture thickens. Remove from heat and stir in butter and food coloring. Serve cool or hot over cheesecake.

This is the same as the raspberry sauce.

Any of these sauces are good on other things. Try them on pudding, pound cakes, and angel food cake. Experiment.

©Connie Hope

Variations:

1. Add 2 ¼ teaspoons pumpkin pie spices when adding other spices.

Make your own pumpkin pie spices. Makes 8 teaspoons.
4 teaspoons cinnamon
2 teaspoons ginger
1 teaspoon allspice
1 teaspoon nutmeg

Mix all ingredients together. Store in airtight container.

Note: After you have used this recipe a couple of times, you can vary it to suit your taste.

2. Substitute ½ cup brown sugar for ½ cup regular sugar.

3. Add 1 cup finely shredded carrots after adding remaining flour.

4. Any and all of the above.

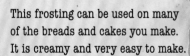

This frosting can be used on many of the breads and cakes you make. It is creamy and very easy to make.

Pumpkin Squares

1 2/3 cups sugar
1 cup oil
4 eggs
1 can (29 oz) solid pumpkin
1 ½ cups flour
½ cup flour
1 teaspoon cinnamon
1 teaspoon salt
1 teaspoon baking soda
2 teaspoons baking powder

Preheat over 350 degrees. Spray with cooking spray a 10 x 15 cooking pan. (I have used two smaller pans) Combine sugar, eggs, and oil. Add pumpkin and mix well. Add 1 ½ cups flour, baking soda, baking powder, and spices. Mix well. Continue to mix pumpkin and add remaining flour. Pour mixture into pan. Bake 30-40 minutes. Check with a knife to make sure it comes out clean. If you are not using the frosting, cool and cut into squares.
Makes 24-30 squares.

Pumpkin Squares   ©Connie Hope

Frosting for Pumpkin Squares
(Optional)
4 oz softened cream cheese
6 Tablespoons margarine, softened
1 teaspoon milk
1 teaspoon vanilla
2 cups confectioner's sugar

Cream together all ingredients while squares cool. Spread frosting on top of squares in pan. Allow to sit, then cut into to square pieces.

Pumpkin Bread

3 cups sugar

1 cup oil

4 eggs, beaten

2 cups canned pumpkin

1 teaspoon baking soda

1 teaspoon baking powder

1 teaspoon clove powder

Pinch of salt

1 teaspoon cinnamon

1 teaspoon nutmeg

3 ¼ cups flour

1 cup nuts *(use pecans, walnuts, or your choice)*

Cream the sugar, oil, and eggs at low speed. Then add the pumpkin, dry ingredients, and nuts. Spray pans. Bake 350 degrees for 60 minutes or until knife comes out clean. Makes either 2 medium size loaves or 4 small loaves.

Pineapple-Zucchini Bread

¾ cup margarine

1 cup sugar

4 eggs

2 teaspoons vanilla

3 cups flour

1 cup chopped walnuts or pecans

2 teaspoons baking powder

1 teaspoon each baking soda, cinnamon

Pinch of salt

1 ½ cups shredded zucchini, clean skin. Do not peel.

1 8 oz can crushed pineapple, well-drained

Cream margarine and sugar until light and airy. Blend in eggs and vanilla. Add combined dry ingredients and mix well. Stir in zucchini and pineapple. Pour into greased loaf pans. Use with 2 medium loaves pan or 4-5 small loaf pans. Bake at 350 degrees for 1 hour 10 minutes for the large loaf and 40-50 minutes for the smaller loaf pans. Check with a knife to make sure it comes out clean. Makes 2 medium size loaves or 4 small loaves.

These two bread recipes are great for gifts over the holidays. I make up many loaves and cover with foil to freeze until I am ready to give them as gifts. *YUM.*

Variations:
Add dates or raisins when you add the nuts.

Always leave room at the top of the pan for the bread to rise.

This is good holiday gift bread. I have given this gift to many friends. Wrap in foil and freeze until ready to bring to friends. Then wrap in plastic and put on a holiday bow.

You can use 2 cups Cranberry-Orange Relish (see index) in place of the orange and 1 cup fresh cranberry in this recipe.

Remember that each oven has its own temperature and you need to check items as they are baking to determine if they are done.

Excellent with soups.

Test the bread's 'doneness' with a clean knife. Put the knife into the bread. If it is done, it will come out clean.

©Connie Hope

Cranberry-Orange Bread

2 cup flour
Pinch of salt
½ teaspoon baking soda
1 cup sugar
1 ½ teaspoon baking powder
1 egg
1 unpeeled orange—cleaned well and cut into eighths
2 Tablespoons margarine and add boiling water to make 1 cup
1 cup walnuts or pecans
1 cup fresh cranberry—put into blender and chop. Set aside

Mix flour, salt, baking soda, sugar, baking powder. Set aside. Put oranges and cranberries in blender with egg. Pulse. Blend until peel is finely chopped. Add nuts to flour mixture, pour in orange/cranberry mixture, butter and water. Mix together. Bake one large and one small or several smaller loaves. Bake 350 degrees for 1 hour 10 minutes for large loaf and 1 hour for smaller loaves. Check with knife several times.

Dilly Casserole Bread

2 ½ cups flour
2 Tablespoons sugar
1 Tablespoon instant minced onions
2 teaspoons dill seed
1 egg
1 ½ teaspoons salt
½ teaspoon baking soda
1 package yeast
1 cup cottage cheese
½ cup water
1 Tablespoon butter

Combine flour, sugar, onion, dill, salt, baking soda, and yeast. In sauce pan, heat cottage cheese, water, and butter until warm. Add egg and warm liquid to flour mixture. Blend at lowest speed until mixture is moist. Beat 3 minutes at medium. By hand stir in remaining flour to form stiff dough. Cover and let rise for 1 hour or until it doubles. Put in medium size casserole. Cover and let rise 30-40 minutes more. Bake 350 degrees, 35 minutes.

Rich Rice Pudding

1 quart milk scalded (heat the milk until it almost boils, stir
  continually so it does not stick to the bottom of the pan.)

½ cup long grain rice

½ cup raisins

3 eggs beaten

½ cup sugar

1 cup evaporated milk

Simmer until rice is cooked.
Beat 3 eggs with ½ cup sugar and 1 cup evaporated milk. Cook mixture for 5
minutes. Stir continually. Put into bowl and sprinkle with cinnamon.

Black Magic Slop Cake

2 cups flour

2 cups sugar

¾ cup cocoa

1 teaspoon baking powder

2 teaspoon baking soda

2 eggs

½ cup oil

1 cup coffee

1 cup milk (or buttermilk)

Grease Bundt or rectangle cake pan. Preheat oven to 350 degrees.
Mix all ingredients together and put in pan. Mixture will be very thin.
Don't panic! Bake at 350 degrees for 35 minutes. Allow to cool.

Frosting

4 oz softened cream cheese

6 Tablespoons margarine, softened

1 teaspoon milk

1 teaspoon vanilla extract

2 cups confectioner's sugar

Mix all ingredients with electric mixer.
Spread frosting on top.

My mother used to make this recipe
all the time. It is creamy and rich.
You will really enjoy it if you love
rice pudding as I do.

Thanks, Mom.

A friend I worked with in 1989
gave me this recipe and I have used
it many times with much success.
Many people have loved it.

Thanks, Cathy.

Buttermilk:

To make buttermilk combine
1 Tablespoon vinegar to 1 cup milk
and let stand for 1 hour.

Lee, a friend from Pennsylvania, gave me this recipe after she had made it for our family. My kids had two pieces each. They loved it! I think you will too.

You can substitute any type of berry in this recipe.

I have used strawberries, boysenberries, and raspberries for this recipe. Any type berry works well.

Berry Delight

1 ¾ cups graham cracker crumbs
6 Tablespoons sugar
½ cup margarine, melted
1 package (8 oz) cream cheese
¼ cup sugar
2 Tablespoons milk
3 ½ cups frozen whipping cream, thawed
2 pints fresh strawberries *(frozen can be used)*
2 packages vanilla instant pudding
3 ¼ cups cold milk

Combine graham crumbs, sugar, and melted margarine. Press into the bottom of a 13 x 9 pan. Chill several hours. Beat cream cheese, ¼ cup sugar, and 2 Tablespoons milk. Fold in ½ of the whipping cream. Put into pan and arrange sliced berries in the mixture. Mix 3 ¼ cups milk with 2 packages of instant pudding. Chill for 2 hours then add to pan with other mixture. Chill Before serving, spread the remaining whipped cream on top. Cut into serving sizes. Garnish with strawberries or berries.

Fruit Yogurt Pie

2 ½ containers (6 oz each or to equal 16 oz) berry yogurt
½ cup crushed berries
1 container (8 oz) frozen whip cream, thawed
1 graham cracker crust *(can use chocolate crust also)*

Add fruit and yogurt and fold in the ¾ frozen whip cream. Blend well and put mixture in the crust. Freeze for 4 hours. Use rest of frozen whip cream on top. Refrigerate.

Fruit Yogurt Pie

The Fruit Cake

2 cups chopped nuts
1 ½ cups pitted dates
1 cup candied cherries
1 cup candied pineapple
½ cup candied oranges
½ cup candied lemons
2 cups sifted flour
Pinch of salt
1 teaspoon baking powder
1 teaspoon ground allspice
½ teaspoon ground nutmeg
1 cup shortening *(I use margarine)*
½ cup sugar
½ cup honey
5 eggs
1/3 cup orange juice
1 cup raisins

Shake nuts, dates, and candied fruit in ¼ cup flour. Mix remaining flour, salt, baking powder and spices. Cream together shortening and sugar; stir in honey. Beat in eggs, one at a time. Add dry ingredients alternately with the orange juice. Stir in the raisins. Pour batter over floured candied mixture and mix well. Pour into 2 large greased and floured loaf pans. You can also use 3-4 smaller loaf pans. Bake at 275 degrees for 2 hours. Check with knife. Remove loaves from pans and cool. Soak several thicknesses of cheesecloth in ¼ cup brandy or your favorite wine and wrap around each loaf. Wrap with aluminum foil. Store in refrigerator for 2 weeks.

The Fruit Cake   ©Connie Hope

People either love fruit cake or they hate it. I have used this recipe for 40 years and those who hate fruit cake like this one. It is not heavy with fruit and the brandy adds the right taste.

I prefer brandy, Drambuie or Grand Marnier. But it could be your choice.

I usually put them in my refrigerator a few weeks before I need to give them as gifts. When I want to give them, I remove the foil and cheesecloth, and wrap in plastic wrap, and add a bow.

Connie's Cooking Tips:

■ Egg whites should be at room temperature before whipping them. Be certain there are no yolks in the whites.

■ Cream, on the other hand, should be chilled before whipping.

■ Substitutions:

If a recipe calls for 1 cup of sour cream, you could substitute 1 cup of cottage cheese. Blend with 1 Tablespoon lemon juice and 1/3 cup buttermilk.

To make buttermilk combine 1 Tablespoon vinegar to 1 cup milk and let stand for 1 hour.

■ Read a recipe through from beginning to end before you start to cook. Make sure that you have all of the needed ingredients and utensils. Then begin your experience of cooking.

■ Assemble all your ingredients on the counter before cooking. I usually measure all the ingredients before I begin cooking. I put out all my utensils, measuring cups, and spoons. Now I am ready.

■ Boiling eggs the best way:
Cover eggs with cold water and a pinch of salt.
Bring the water to a full boil.
Boil for 1 minute then remove the pot from heat and cover.
Leave eggs in the water covered for 9-10 minutes.
Drain eggs and place in ice water to cool.
The shells should come off easily.

©Connie Hope

Jelly

Jellies are made from the juice of fruit. Jelly is a clear or translucent sparkling gel that is firm enough to hold its shape when removed from the glass. It is sweet and 'fruitie' made through the addition of sugar and pectin to edible liquid. It is boiled until it starts to gel. The gel point is when the thickened sauce will stay on the spoon when it is turned on its side. (See Appendix for gel point or spoon drip test.) It is simply sweetened and jelled fruit juice. Generally, jelly contains no pieces of fruit, although specialty jellies, like pepper jelly, may include pieces of jalapeno or other peppers suspended in the gel. The hot mixture is usually strained either through cheesecloth, a "food mill" or strainer. This will make the mixture clearer, smoother and free of pits or seeds. Jelly is not something that can be rushed. Please don't think that you can squeeze the cheese- cloth to hurry the process. This squeeze will tend to cloud the jelly. Jelly-making is an art and art takes time. I love to made jelly and create a new taste treat. It takes a little time, but it is well worth the reward of many praises.

Mango Jelly

2.2 pounds of hard mango slices *(should not be ripe)*
   About 5-6 mangos depending on size
1 ¾ cups of water
3 cups of sugar
Juice of one lemon
1 envelope of pectin (more if needed)

Put mango chunks or slices in a large pot. Add water and cook until fork tender. Put mango and water in a food processor and pulse. Put mango pulp back in large pot. Add sugar and lemon juice. Cook on medium heat until boiling. Add one envelope of pectin. Boil for at least 5 minutes; stir continually, check gel point. *(see appendix) If not gelled enough, add more pectin)* In sterilized jars, add mixture to about ½ inch from top. Do not overfill. Make sure rim of bottle is clean. Put lid and ring on. Water bath for 15 minutes. Makes 6 -8 half pints

©Connie Hope

See 'How to Cut a Mango"
(see appendix)

Serve with:

Ice cream
Puddings
Pies
Cakes

Toast
Muffins
Ham
Chicken
Pork Chops

I use this on a cream cheese block for an appetizer. It is fast and delicious .(See index for Appetizers)

Serve with:
Toast
Muffins
Cream cheese
Ham
Pork Chops

I like to make sure the color is a rich green. If you want to darken color, add several drops of food coloring.

To clean the seeds and veins from jalapeno peppers, use a teaspoon to scrape. Always use rubber gloves.

This has more of the jalapeno peppers than the others and uses red peppers rather than green, which adds to the color of the jelly. It is a little spicier than the other jalapeno jellies.

Jalapeno Jelly *(see appetizers)*

3 jalapeno peppers

4 green bell peppers

1 cup white vinegar

5 cups sugar

1 envelope pectin *(may need ½ envelope more, check sheeting of liquid on spoon. See appendix-gel test)*

4-6 drops of green food coloring *(Optional)*

Remove seeds and thick skin, then chop green peppers in food processor. Cut, clean, remove seeds, and chop jalapeno peppers in food processor. Put peppers, vinegar, and sugar in a large pot and bring to a boil at medium heat for approximately 7-10 minutes. Remove from the heat and add pectin. Stir. Bring back to a full boil for 1-2 minutes, stir continually. Pour into sterilized half pint jars. Make sure that it is ½ inch from top. Clean jar top of excess, seal with lid and ring. Water bath for 15 minutes. Makes about 6-10 half pints.

Jalapeno Jelly #2

10 jalapeno peppers, cut and seeds removed

(You may want to use gloves. If you touch your eyes with your fingers, it will smart)

2 red bell peppers, medium

1 ½ cups vinegar, distilled

5 cups sugar

1/3 cup lemon juice (use either fresh lemons or bottle juice)

1 envelope of liquid pectin (may need ½ pouch more)

10 drips green food coloring (optional)

Put jalapeno peppers and red bell peppers in food processor and chop until fine. Combine chopped peppers, vinegar, sugar, and lemon juice. Bring to a boil for 10 minutes, stirring continually. Stir in pectin and food coloring. Boil again. Stir continually for over one minute. Skim off any foam. Pour liquid into sterilized jars and seal with lids and rings. Water bath for 15 minute. Makes about 6-10 half pints.

©Connie Hope

(Cattley) Guava Jelly

1 ½ cups guava juice
1 Tablespoon lemon juice
1 ¼ cups sugar
2 pouches pectin (have extra on hand)

To Prepare Guava Juice

Remove pointed end of Cattley guava and rinse. Put in pot and cover with water. Boil for 5 minutes. Use a potato masher on the fruit and continue to boil for a few more minutes. Press though a cheesecloth bag that strains the fruit. (I usually hang a cheesecloth bag from a cabinet handle and put a large bowl underneath.) Do not squeeze the bag to get extra juice as it will tend to make the jelly cloudy. It will take 4-5 hours or overnight to get all the juice.

To Prepare the Jelly

Measure Cattley guava juice and bring to a boil. For each 1 ½ cup guava juice, add 1¼ cups sugar, 1 Tablespoon lemon juice and 2 pouches pectin. Bring juice to a boil for 6 minutes. Stir continually. Remove from heat and add pectin. Bring back to a boil for 3 minutes and stir test for gel stage. Put into sterilized jars. Make sure rim is cleaned and ½ inch from top. Seal with lid and rings. Water bath for 20 minutes. Makes 2-3 plus half pints

Guava is a small tree we have in Florida. There was not enough fruit on our tree for me to make jelly. I had seen several Cattley guava trees that had fruit near the mall. I picked the fruit from these trees. Luckily, I did not get arrested.

Cheesecloth can be purchased in most stores. I just use a square and form a jelly bag to put the fruit in. I then tie it with string.

Guava is a fruit that is the size of a lemon. The Cattley Guava has a much smaller fruit about the size of a small cherry. This recipe can be used for either.

The guava does not have a great deal of natural pectin. Pick some green fruit which has more of the natural pectin. The last batch I did I had to redo and add more pectin to make the jelly set correctly. Always have an extra pouch or two of liquid pectin on hand.

I collected a gallon size plastic bag that yielded about 6 cups of guava juice. I multiplied this recipe by 4.

©Connie Hope

Serve with:

Lamb Roast
Lamb Chops
Ham

These two recipes use apple juice and mint leaves, which make a sweet, apple-mint flavored jelly.

Mint Jelly (using mint extract)

2 cups apple juice
1 ½ cups sugar
1 pouch pectin
1 teaspoon mint extract
green food coloring

In a large pot, combine apple juice and sugar. Bring to a rolling boil for 4 minutes. Stir continually. Remove from heat and add pectin and stir. Return to a boil for 1 minute. When mixture has started to gel, add the mint extract and food coloring. Continue to boil for 1 minute. Pour into sterilized jars. Clean top of jar and make sure it is ½ inch from top of jar. Water bath for 15 minutes. Makes about 3-4 half pints

©Connie Hope

On the following pages you will learn to make mint jelly using vinegar, which has more of a tangy taste.

Mint Jelly (using fresh mint)

4 cups of apple juice
2 cups minced mint leaves
1 pouch pectin
6 drops of green food coloring (more if you like a darker green color)
4 ½ cups sugar

In a large pot combine apple juice, mint, pectin and food coloring. Bring mixture to a full boil stirring sugar in gradually. Bring again to a full boil. Boil hard for 1 minute, stirring continually. Remove from heat and remove mint leaves. Skim off any foam. Pour into sterilized jars. Make sure that the top of the jar is clean and you have left about ½ inch from the top of the jar. Seal with lid and ring. Water bath for 15 minutes. Makes 5-6 half pints

Mint Jelly (using vinegar for more tang)

1 cup fresh mint leave, firmly packed

½ cup apple cider vinegar

1 cup water

3 ½ cups sugar

4-5 drops green food coloring (use more if you like a darker green)

1 pouch liquid fruit pectin

Wash the mint and drain. In order to get the flavor from the mint, bruise the mint in a pot with a heavy glass tumbler (smash it). Add vinegar, water, and sugar. Bring to full boil, stirring continually until the sugar has dissolved. Add green coloring and pectin and return to a full boil. Boil hard for 1 minute, stirring continually. Remove from heat. Skim off any foam. Pour mixture into sterilized jars. Make sure the rim is clean and the jelly is at least ½ inch from the top. Seal with lid and rim. Water bath for 15 minutes. Makes 3-4 half pints

Mint Jelly

2 cups water

1 cup apple cider vinegar

1 cup mint leaves

6 cups sugar

2 pouches of fruit pectin

4-5 drops green food coloring

Combine water, vinegar, mint leaves, and sugar. Bring to a boil. Add fruit pectin. Bring to a boil for 1 minute. Remove leaves. Pour mixture into sterilized jars. Make sure the rim is clean and the jelly is at least ½ inches from the top. Seal with lid and rim. Water bath for 15 minutes. Makes 4-5 plus half pint jars

©Connie Hope

Serve with:
Lamb
Ham
Pork Chops

Please note: With apple-vinegar based jelly, the setting point can be detected when the foam calms down somewhat.

Make sure you leave plenty of room in your pot for the jelly to foam up. You don't want to have to clean your stove.

This mint jelly recipe can be used with several different herbs. You can expand the recipe to such herbs as:

| Basil | 1 Cup |
| Rosemary leaves | ½ Cup |

Or use your imagination and try something new.

Serve with:

Toast
Muffins
Rolls
Ice cream
Pudding

Can be used with cream cheese as an appetizer.

Sea grapes are available along many shores on the East Coast where the temperatures do not fall below 32 degrees.

This jelly is very mild with a wonderful light taste.

Sea Grape Jelly

1 quart sea grape juice

5 Tablespoons lemon or lime juice

1 pouch pectin *(may need a little more depending on how ripe the sea grapes are when picked)*

5 cups sugar

To prepare Sea Grape Juice:

Wash sea grapes
Measure sea grapes: 1 cup water to 2 cups sea grapes.
Put in large pot and bring to a boil.
Mash often with a potato masher and continue to boil.
Fruit is reduced to a soft pulp that takes about 30 minutes.
Drain through a jelly bag or cheesecloth. Do Not Squeeze.
  (Jelly will be cloudy if you squeeze.) It takes at least 4
  hours or overnight to drip.

To Prepare the Sea Grape Jelly:

Place one quart of juice in a kettle at high heat. Add lemon or lime juice and pectin and bring to a boil. Stir in sugar and return to a boil for 1-2 minutes. Stir continually. Remove from heat and skim foam. Pour into ½ pint sterilized jars. Leave ½ inch at top of jar. Seal with lid and ring. Water bath for 15 minutes. Makes 3-4 half pints.

©Connie Hope

Rose Hips Jelly

4 quarts ripe rose hips (16 cups)

2 quarts water

½ cup lemon juice

1 package fruit pectin (have extra on hand)

5 ½ cups sugar

Simmer rose hips in water until soft. Mash with potato masher and strain through cheesecloth. It will take 4 hours plus to drip thought cheesecloth. Should make about 3 cups of rose hip juice. *(It will vary)* Put juice into a pot and add lemon juice and pectin. Stir mixture until it is at a hard boil. Stir sugar in all at once. Bring to a full boil and boil for 1 minute. Stir continually. Remove from heat and skim any foam. Pour into jars and water bath for 25 minutes.

Rose Hips Tea—3 ways
1. You can buy them at your local specialty store
2. Fresh rose hips
3. Dried rose hips

Fresh Rose hips

3-5 fresh rose hips, chopped

1 cup boiling water

Put fresh rose hips in a tea pot. Add 1 cup boiling water. Allow to brew for 10-15 minutes if you like it mild or 30 minutes for strong tea. Filter thought a strainer into cup. Reheat and add sweetener to taste.

Dried Rose hips

Spread rose hips on cookie tray and allow to partially dry. When the skins start to shrivel, remove the seeds. Cut in half. Use a spoon to remove the seeds. Let the rose hips completely dry before storing. Keep in a small sealed plastic bag. For tea, add 2 teaspoons dried rose hips to 1 cup of boiling water. Brew for 5 minutes, strain, add sweetener as desired.

©Connie Hope

©Connie Hope

Remove the blossom remnants from the rose hips. Wash them before you put them in water to cook.

If the rose hip is too small and hard, there will be very little flesh. Generally, the plumper the rose hips, the better the taste and the better the jelly.

Rose hips are the cherry sized red fruits on the rose bush. They are left behind after the bloom has died.

The rose hips are tastier if left on the bush until after the first frost, however, if the color is right and they feel ripe, pick them when you are ready to make jelly.

Don't use aluminum utensils or pans when cooking the rose hips.

Rose hips are valued for their high concentration of vitamin C.

Rose hips will keep on the shelf in the refrigerator for several months or frozen them in a sealed bag for up to 6 months.

Rose Hips

©Connie Hope

Rose Hips Jelly

©Connie Hope

Jam

Jams are thick, sweet spreads that will hold their shape, but are less firm than jelly. Jams are made of crushed or chopped fruits or the pulp of fruit. These fruit juices are mixed with sugar and boiled rapidly until thick and a smooth consistency. Jams are stronger in fruit flavors and solid in appearance. This is produced by using mashed or chopped fruit pulp and juices. The fruit is more visible and is thicker than jelly. Jams can be puree of fruit or have a soft, pulpy appearance, but do not contain large chunks of fruit. Jelly is filtered and strained so no visual chunks of fruit appear, only clear gel.

©Connie Hope

Kiwi Jam

4 cups mashed kiwi (use a food processor)

5-6 cups sugar

4 Tablespoons lemon juice

2 pouches liquid pectin

Combine kiwi, sugar, and lemon and bring to a boil. Add pectin and boil for one minute. Put into canning jars and seal. Water bath for 15 minutes. Makes 6 half pint jars.

I have always loved the flavor of kiwi. This makes a great flavored jam.

Persimmon Jam

3 lbs ripe persimmons

7 cups sugar

Juice of 2 lemons (fresh is best)

1 pouch liquid pectin

Wash, peel, and seed the persimmons or if very ripe, cut in half and scoop out the pulp. Mash pulp and put persimmon pulp in a large pot. Add sugar and lemon juice and mix well. Bring slowly to a boil over high heat until sugar is dissolved. Boil hard for 1 minute. Remove pot from heat Stir in pectin and return to a full boil. Put into sterilized jars and water bath for 20 minutes. Makes 5-6 half pint jars.

Always have an extra pectin pouch available in case the jam does not thicken enough.

Try the gel point test—see Appendix

See Appendix on how to cut a mango.

Variations are:

Add a stick of cinnamon and 2 cloves for flavor

Substitute lime juice for lemon juice

This can be used when making Plum Sauce-see index.

Serve with:
Ice cream and puddings
Cake
Pancakes

It is complementary with:
Pork or ham
Turkey
Chicken

©Connie Hope

Mango Jam

4 cups mango pulp
¼ cup lemon juice
6 cups sugar
1 pouch of liquid pectin

Wash, peel, and cut mangos into cubes. Mash with a potato masher or put in a food processor. In a pot add fruit and lemon juice. Heat to a boil, stirring constantly, and add the sugar. Return to a full boil (that can't be stirred down). Remove from heat and add the pectin. Return to heat and boil for 2 minutes. Skim off any foam. Put into sterilized jars and water bath for 15 minutes. Makes 4-6 half pints

Plum Jam

2 quarts tart plums, remove pits and chop
6 cups sugar
1 ½ cups water
¼ cup lemon juice
1 pouch liquid pectin

Combine all ingredients. Bring to a boil, stirring continually until all sugar dissolves. Cook rapidly for at least 30 minutes. Stir continually. Remove from heat and add liquid pectin. Return to boil. Put in sterilized jars, make sure rim is clean, put on lid and ring, and water bath for 20 minutes. Makes 5-7 half pints

Blueberry Jam

4 ½ cups fresh crushed blueberries
2 Tablespoons lemon juice
7 cups sugar
2 pouches of liquid pectin. *(May need another pouch)*

Remove stems and crush berries to measure 4 ½ cups. Put berries in a large pot. Add lemon juice and sugar and mix well. Heat on high. Bring to a full boil and boil hard for 1 minute. Remove from the heat, then add the pectin and stir. Skim any foam off the top. Put into sterilized jar and seal with lid and rim. Water bath for 15 minutes. Makes 5-6 half pints

Fig Jam

2 quarts chopped fresh figs *(around 5 pounds)* **or dried figs** *(see side notes)*
6 cups of sugar
¾ cup water
¼ cup lemon juice
(You may need 1 pouch of liquid fruit pectin)

Prepare figs: Cover with water about ¼ cup, boil for 5 minutes then let stand for 10 minutes. Drain water and chop. Combine figs, sugar, and water in a large pot. Bring to a boil. Stir continually until all sugar dissolves. Cook over medium heat until thick. Stir continually. If it does not thicken, add pectin and continue to cook for another few minutes, but it usually is thick. Add lemon juice and continue heating for 1 minute. Put mixture in sterilized jars making sure that the rim is cleaned and the mixture is down ½ inch. Seal with lid and rim. Water bath for 15 minutes. Makes 6-10 half pints

Fig Jam   ©Connie Hope

8 cups = 2 quarts
(Recipe can be cut in half)

My favorite is to place the fig jam in a small cup and use a knife with a variety of cheese squares.

It is also tasty with cream cheese as an appetizer.

It is complementary with ham.

Baked brie is great with fig jam on it. It is thick like a paste and has a great taste.
Yum!

If you can't find fresh figs, I have used dried. So you need to improvise a little.

When using dried figs, I cut the recipe in thirds and didn't add as much sugar. Then add pectin. It is more like a paste than a jam.

This is great if you are serving
steak or baked tofu.

Serve with:
Steak
Pork
Sausages
Baked tofu

This is excellent with steak or
any kind of fish. The ginger adds
a nice taste to the tomatoes.

Serve with:

Pork
Ham
Steak
Fish and Shrimp

Spiced Tomato Jam

2 ¼ pounds ripe tomatoes
½ cup fresh lemon juice
Grated peel of one lemon
½ teaspoon cinnamon
¼ teaspoon allspice
¼ teaspoon cloves
1 pouch liquid fruit pectin
4 ½ cups sugar

Put tomatoes in boiling water for 3 minutes to loosen skin. Peel, core, remove
seeds, and chop tomatoes in food processor. Put tomatoes in a large pot and
bring to a boil. Turn down and simmer for 10 minutes. Drain and measure
3 cups of tomato pulp into a pot. Add lemon juice, lemon peel, spices, and
pectin. Mix well. Bring to a full boil, stirring continually. Add sugar all at once.
Bring to a full boil and stir continually for one minute. Remove from heat. Put
mixture in sterilized jars. Clean top rim and make sure ½ inch is remaining
in jar. Seal with lid and rim. Water bath for 20 minutes. Makes 6-7 half pints.

Tomato-Ginger Jam

5 pounds fresh tomatoes
1 ½ cups sugar
1 ½ cups fresh lemon juice
1/3 cup fresh garlic, thinly sliced or chopped
1/3 cup fresh ginger, finely chopped or minced
½ teaspoon salt

Peel, seed, and chop tomatoes. Place in stainless steel pan. Bring to a boil,
reduce to medium simmer heat. Cook for 30 minutes. Stir occasionally. Put
in sterilized jars. Clean top and make sure ½ remaining at top. Seal with lid
and rim. Water bath for 20 minutes. Makes about 7-8 half pints.

©Connie Hope

Marmalade

Marmalade is a soft jelly, often citrus-based. It includes the chunks of flesh and often the peel of the fruit is suspended throughout the transparent jelly base. The sweetness of the jelly is offset by the bitterness or tartness of the peel. Some products that are called marmalade (onion and tomato marmalades, for example) are actually misnamed jams and preserves.

©Connie Hope

Citrus Marmalade

Peels from 2 grapefruit, sliced thin
Peels from 2 oranges, sliced thin
Peels from 1 lemon, sliced thin
Pulp from 2 grapefruits about 1 ½ cups
Pulp from 2 oranges about ¾ cup
Pulp from 1 lemon about ½ cup
4 cups water
4-5 cups sugar (This depends on how sweet you like your marmalade. I prefer mine a little on the tart side so I use only 4 cups sugar.)
1 package fruit pectin (may need additional)

Combine fruit peels, 4 cups water, 4 cups sugar, and fruit pulp. Bring to a boil for 10 minutes stirring continually. Cool, cover, and refrigerate for a day. Put back on the stove and bring to a boil. Stir to dissolve the sugar. Reduce heat and cook for 45 minutes or until peels are tender and mixture has thickened. Skim off any foam that has appeared. Put mixture in hot jars leaving ½ inch at top. Water bath for 20 minutes. Makes about 5-6 half pint jelly jars.

This complements ham or pork chops.

As you are cooking the ham or ham slice, put marmalade on the outside about 15 minutes before done and it will have a golden crust.

This marmalade is great on toast and English muffins.

©Connie Hope

©Connie Hope

Kumquat Marmalade

3 cups chopped kumquats

1 cup water

Juice from one lemon equal to ½ cup *(use more lemons if needed)*

1 pouch liquid fruit pectin

6 ½ cups sugar

Cut the kumquats to resemble a cartwheel and remove seeds. Slice very thin. Combine kumquats, water, lemon juice, and pectin in a pot. Add sugar and bring to a hard boil. Cool the mixture for one minute. If you want, you can add a few drops of orange food color. Invert jars until marmalade begins to set to keep peels evenly distributed in the jar. Invert again if needed. Pour into sterilized jars and water bath. Makes about 3-4 half pint jars.

This makes a tart marmalade, but it is good with ham and pork chops.

Serve with:

Toast or English muffins
Ham
Pork chops
Shrimp
Baked tofu

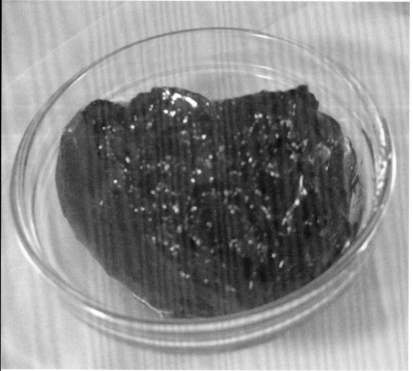

Kumquat Marmalade   ©Connie Hope

Orange-Carrot Marmalade

6 large carrots

3 oranges

1 lemon

Sugar *(see below)*

1 pouch pectin

Cut the carrot in thin strips. Steam carrots until tender. Cut oranges and skin in small pieces. Make sure that you collect the juice from the orange. *(I suggest you cut the orange up in a low bowl.)* Grate the rind of the lemon. Measure the carrots, oranges, and lemons. For each cup of fruit, add a cup of sugar. Add one pouch of liquid pectin. Simmer the mixture from 45 minutes to an hour or until the sugar has dissolved and the mixture has thickened. Stir occasionally. Put in sterilized jars and seal with lid and rim. Make sure rim is clean and mixture ½ inch from top. Water bath for 20 minutes. Makes 3-5 half pint jars.

Carrot Marmalade

2 pounds carrots, sliced

5 cups of sugar

4 lemons, use the juice and cut up the rinds of 2 lemons

¾ cup chopped nuts *(I prefer pecans, but whatever is your favorite nut will do.)*

The nuts are optional

Steam the sliced carrots until tender, then mash with a potato masher. Add sugar and the juice from the lemons. Add the rind of 2 of the lemons. Cook for 20-30 minutes. Stir continually. Remove from heat and add the nuts (optional). Pour into sterilized jars. Clean the rim and make sure the mixture is at least ½ inch down. Seal with lid and ring and water bath for 20 minutes. Makes 3-5 ½ pint jars.

Suggestions:

Baked ham: Just before it is done, spread the marmalade on the outside of the ham. Bake another 10-15 minutes.

Serve with:
Pork chops or ham.

It also makes a nice taste with chicken salad on a sandwich or in a salad.

Also good is adding spices for a more tangy taste.

½ teaspoon ground cloves
or
½ teaspoon allspice
or
½ teaspoon cinnamon

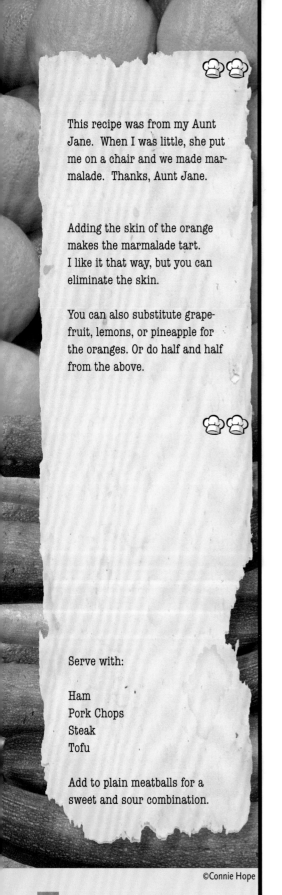

This recipe was from my Aunt Jane. When I was little, she put me on a chair and we made marmalade. Thanks, Aunt Jane.

Adding the skin of the orange makes the marmalade tart. I like it that way, but you can eliminate the skin.

You can also substitute grapefruit, lemons, or pineapple for the oranges. Or do half and half from the above.

Serve with:

Ham
Pork Chops
Steak
Tofu

Add to plain meatballs for a sweet and sour combination.

©Connie Hope

Orange Marmalade

4 oranges (about 2 cups) Make sure skin is clean.

3 lemons thinly sliced (about 1 ½ cups)

2 cups water or orange juice *(I like the orange juice because it adds more flavor)*

1 cup sugar for each cup of fruit

1 pouch liquid fruit pectin *(Always have an extra on hand)*

Peel skin from lemon and orange with vegetable peeler. Set the peels aside *(Chop and add to orange juice to soak.)* Peel off the remaining white rind with your hands. Cut the orange and lemon into thin slices. *(Use a low bowl or pan. You want to make sure you catch all that great juice!)* Remove the center or core as it is bitter. Chop the slices a bit. Put the rinds and liquid in a pot and bring to a boil. Simmer for 20-30 minutes. Stir occasionally. Add the fruit, rinds, and the remaining liquid to the pot. Add sugar and pectin; bring to a full boil for 1-2 minutes. Put in sterilized jar and water bath for 15 minutes. Makes 3-4 half pint jars.

Zucchini Marmalade

2 pounds zucchini *(Clean outside of zucchini, then grate)*

2 teaspoons grated lemon zest (about 2 lemons)

Juice of 2 lemons (about ¼ - 1/3 cup)

1 can 12-14 oz crushed pineapple *(drain for extended time)*

4 cups sugar

2 Tablespoons crystallized ginger, finely chopped

1 pouch liquid fruit pectin. *(I always keep this on hand. If you see that the marmalade is not thickening, add ½ pouch and bring to a boil.)*

In a saucepan, mix zucchini, lemon juice, lemon rind, and crushed pineapple. Bring mixture to a boil, reduce heat. Cook for 20 minutes. Stir in the ginger and stir while adding the sugar. Add the pectin and return the mixture to a boil. Stir and bring to a full rapid boil for 2 minutes. Remove from stove. Skim foam off the top. Make sure rim is clean and mixture is at least ½ from top. Pack in sterile jars and seal with lid and rim. Water bath for 20 minutes. Makes 4-5 half pint jars.

Lemon Marmalade (Lime Marmalade)

3 lemons (or limes)

1 grapefruit

One pouch fruit pectin

4-4 ½ cups sugar *(This is very tart, so if you like things on the sweeter side use the 4 ½ cups of sugar)*

4 cups of water

Wash all fruit. Take a potato peeler and remove the skin of the lemons and grapefruit. *(I always remove the skin first then cut up the fruit. It's just easier).* Slice the skin into thin strips. *(Make sure it is thin)* Cut lemon and grapefruit in half and squeeze juice and pulp out. Remove seeds. Place rinds, pulp and juice, water and pectin in a pot. Bring to a boil. Skim off foam. Add sugar. Stir until dissolved and bring to a slow boil. Put in sterile jars and put lid and rim on. Make sure rim is clean and mixture is at least ½ inch from top. Makes 3-4 half pint jars.

Variation:

Ginger Lemon Marmalade:
Add 1 Tablespoon of finely chopped crystallized ginger when you add the sugar and continue following the recipe.

Spiced Clove Lemon Marmalade:
Add ½ teaspoon of ground cloves after the mixture has come to a full boil.

Cinnamon Lemon Marmalade:
Add one cinnamon stick when you add the sugar then boil.
Remove the cinnamon stick before you process the marmalade.

©Connie Hope

Serve with:
Fish
Ham
Toast and English Muffins

This is really great with any fish.

©Connie Hope

These variations are fun to try. They are different in taste and you might really like their difference.

Enjoy!

Serve with:
 Thick crusty bread or
 toasted rye or
 pumpernickel

Try this also. It's fantastic!

Pumpkin biscuits:

1 ½ cups flour
3 teaspoons baking powder
1 teaspoon salt
¼ cup sugar
1 teaspoon cinnamon
½ teaspoon cinnamon & nutmeg
¼ teaspoon allspice
1/3 cup cold butter
¾ cup pureed pumpkin
¾ cup milk
Preheat oven 450 degrees

Stir in all dry ingredients.
Cut in butter until crumbly.
Stir in pumpkin and milk to form a
soft dough. Roll out on floured surface
½ inch thick Cut out biscuits with
small cutter. Place on greased baking
sheet. Bake 450 degrees
for 15 minutes.

Makes about 24 biscuits.
Also good with:
 Pork Chops and Ham

Pumpkin Marmalade

4 cups pumpkin (either cut into chunks or scoop out)
   (See appendix on how to cut and cook a pumpkin.)
4 cups sugar
2 lemons
2 oranges
1 pouch pectin

Cut one medium pumpkin, remove seed, peel, and dice in small pieces to measure 4 cups. Mix pumpkin and sugar together in a large bowl. Stir well to dissolve sugar, cover, and let sit overnight in refrigerator. Next day remove the pumpkin pieces from the juice with a slotted spoon and set aside. Cook juice over high heat bring to a boil. Reduce to medium heat and cook for 20 minutes. Remove the outer rind 'zest' of the oranges and lemons and put 'zest' aside. Remove all bitter white membrane and any seeds. Grind zest and fruit together in a food processor. Add pumpkin, citrus fruits, and rind to boiling liquid. Add pectin and gently boil together for 1 ½ hours until the marmalade thickens and pumpkin is translucent.   Stir frequently. Remove from heat. Let marmalade cool and skim foam off on top. Put into sterilized jars. Make sure mixture is at least ½ inch from top of jar. Seal with rim and top. Water bath for 20 minutes. Makes 4-5 half pint jars.

Pumpkin Marmalade   ©Connie Hope

Odds and Ends

There are some recipes that just didn't fit into the categories of my book. I created an 'Odds and Ends' section to accommodate them. These recipes were important so I needed to fit them somewhere for you to enjoy in this book rather than my second book.

This is an excellent salmon dish and the only main course recipe I have included.

©Connie Hope

Spice-Rubbed Salmon

1 Tablespoon brown sugar

1 teaspoon garlic powder

1 teaspoon dried oregano *(or use fresh oregano from your garden)*

1 teaspoon ground cumin

1 teaspoon chili powder

1 teaspoon paprika

½ teaspoon salt *(divided into ¼ and ¼)*

4 medium fillets of salmon, skinned (about 6 oz each)

Cooking spray

Combine all ingredients except salmon. Stir gently. Rub evenly over the fish. Place fish on a pan that is coated with cooking spray. Broil for 8-9 minutes until flaky. Test several times with a fork. Serve with a garnish of mint leaves.

Serve with:
Cucumber Relish
(see index for relishes)

©Connie Hope

A girlfriend served me this and I asked for the recipe.

It is different and very thirst quenching.

I make this when my basil is tall and starting to go to seed.

I have used Crystal Light® powder or small, frozen can of lemonade.

©Connie Hope

I use light cranberry juice as it has fewer calories.

I prefer to use either a citrus or mandarin orange vodka, but use your imagination and try something new.

This was served at a holiday party and I liked it and asked for the recipe.
Thanks, Jim and Karen.

Count your drinks!

Basil Lemonade

1 cup water

Also 3 cups cold water

1 cup sugar *(I have used sugar substitute, but check measurements)*

1 cup fresh basil leaves, packed firmly

2 cups ice

Frozen lemonade, small can or packet powdered lemonade

¼ cup lemon juice *(I love it very tart so I add a little more)*

In a small saucepan, bring 1 cup water and sugar to a boil over medium heat. Cook until the sugar dissolves, about 5 minutes. Remove the saucepan from the heat. Add fresh basil leaves, cover and let stand 30 minutes. Fill a pitcher with 2 cups ice. Strain the sugar syrup into the pitcher. Discard the basil. Stir in 3 cups cold water and packet or can of lemonade. Makes about 6-7 cups.

Cosmopolitan Punch

2 cups vodka

1 ½ cups Cointreau (an orange-flavored liqueur)

1 ½ cups cranberry juice

¾ cup fresh lime juice

½ cup water or club soda

Mix and chill in refrigerator. Makes about 6 cups
Serve in a punch bowl or glass pitcher with slices of lime.

Mint Fresh Tropical Drink

2 large handfuls of fresh mint greens

2 ½ cups water

1 cup sugar (can use sugar substitute, check measurements)

Juice from 4 oranges

Juice from 2 lemons

1 1/3 cup bourbon whiskey and crushed ice

Bring mint, water, and sugar to a boil and add the juices. Remove from heat and let steep for 5-10 minutes. Strain liquid and chill. Add 1 1/3 cups of your favorite bourbon to juices and pour over full glass of crushed ice. Garnish with orange slice. Makes about 5 cups

©Connie Hope

Basic Strata

12 slices bread, remove crust and cube
1   8 oz package shredded cheese, any type
4   cups milk
8   eggs, beaten
1   teaspoon dry mustard is best, but I have used jarred mustard also.
2   Tablespoons minced onion
Salt and pepper to taste
Dash of cayenne pepper
3   Tablespoons butter

Spray a 9 x 13 casserole dish. *(I like to use a fancy one.)* Spread bread, then cheese. Beat milk, eggs, dry mustard, onion, and spices. Pour over cheese and bread mix. Dot with butter. Refrigerate overnight. Bake one hour at 350 degrees. Serve hot.

Variations: You can use one, two, or three of these in one strata.
Have fun!

Spinach Strata: Add 2 packages frozen chopped, thawed and drained spinach or use 1 bag of fresh spinach.

Mushroom Strata: Add 1 cup mushrooms to the strata or add this to any of the other strata.

Broccoli Strata: Add 1 package chopped, frozen broccoli, cooked well and drained or 2 heads fresh broccoli cooked, drained.

Sausage Strata: Add 1 ½ cups sausage, cooked and crumbled.

Bacon Strata: Add 3-4 slices bacon very crispy and crumbled.

Tomato Strata: Add a can of stewed tomatoes with spices and herbs.

Other variations:

Zucchini
Crab
Leeks-2 chopped
Bleu Cheese
Feta Cheese
Asparagus—steamed
Chicken
Ham

Thank you, Lisa, for this great recipe.

You can use any type of cheese you like or make it 4 oz each of two cheeses: Cheddar, Swiss, Mozzarella.

Using this basic recipe, you can add whatever you like to zest it up.

I have included a few variations, but the choice is endless. Experiment and create your own. Let me know your creations.

You can substitute 2 - 8 oz. cartons of egg substitute.

My daughter is vegan and I have even used the egg powder substitute, which works great. It should be baked for another 10 minutes.

I use this if I am having guests for brunch or just a group over for a breakfast.

Also you can add :
¼ cup fresh basil
¼ teaspoon thyme
½ cup red peppers

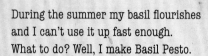

During the summer my basil flourishes and I can't use it up fast enough. What to do? Well, I make Basil Pesto.

Serve with:
Pasta
Baked potatoes
Appetizers with toast
Over fish or chicken

It is a recipe that you can change to your taste. Most pesto calls for Parmesan cheese, but if you like Romano better, then substitute.

I freeze my pesto. Omit the cheese until you serve it. I put it in ice cube trays, let it freeze, then pop it out into a freezer bag. It will store for several months.

My favorite is 'pesto on pasta.' I pop out 2-3 ice cubes of pesto and put them in a pot. I use a little wine and a little water and heat. Make any type of pasta *(I like bow ties best.)* and put your pesto on top. Add your cheese.

Viola!

Basil Pesto

2 cups fresh basil leaves, packed firmly
1/3 cup pine nuts, walnuts, pecans, or whatever
3 medium sized cloves of garlic minced *(If you really like garlic add more to your taste.)*
½ cup extra virgin olive oil
½ cup, freshly grated cheese *(Parmesan or Romano or whatever)*
Salt and fresh ground pepper *(I use a lime pepper made by Jane's Krazy Mixed-Up Seasonings®, see appendix)*

Combine basil and nuts in a food processor and pulse. Add garlic and pulse. Slowly add the olive oil in a steady stream. Scrape sides and pulse again. Add the cheese if you are not going to freeze the pesto. Salt and fresh ground pepper to taste. If you are freezing, put into ice cube trays or in an airtight container and refrigerate.

Pesto can be served on many things, so use your imagination.

Here are just a few ideas:

■ **On pizza in place of or in addition to the red sauce.**
■ **Add to an Alfredo sauce.**
■ **Stir into mashed potatoes.**
■ **Stir into risotto.**
■ **Put a dollop on soup.**
■ **Combine with mayonnaise on sandwich or toppings.**
■ **Add to scrambled eggs or fold into omelets.**

Basil Pesto   ©Connie Hope

Cilantro Pesto

1 bunch fresh cilantro

4-5 cloves garlic, minced

1 Tablespoon white wine vinegar

¼ cup grated parmesan cheese

½ teaspoon cayenne pepper

½ cup nuts (pine nuts, walnuts or pecans)

Salt and fresh pepper to taste

½ cup olive oil

Combine cilantro, garlic, vinegar, parmesan cheese, cayenne pepper, nuts, and salt and pepper in a food processor and pulse. Add 1/4 cup of the olive oil at the top slowly and pulse. Then add the remaining olive oil and blend until smooth. Pour over pasta or whatever you are serving, or put in ice cubes trays to freeze.

Lemon-Artichoke Pesto

¼ cup fresh cilantro, chopped

6-8 garlic cloves

4 Tablespoons lemon juice-fresh is best

½ teaspoon cayenne pepper

1 cup nuts (pine nuts, walnuts or pecans)

1 cup olive oil

Salt and fresh round pepper to taste

1 can artichoke hearts, drained and chopped

½ cup parmesan cheese

Combine cilantro, garlic, lemon juice, cayenne pepper, nuts, olive oil, and salt and pepper in a food processor. Pulse until smooth. Gently stir in chopped artichokes and parmesan cheese.(If you are freezing, do not put in the cheese) Serve on pasta or melba toast for appetizers.

Pesto can be made of herbs other than basil. Why not try it with cilantro or mint or use your imagination?

If you like garlic, add more or if you dislike it, take some away

©Connie Hope

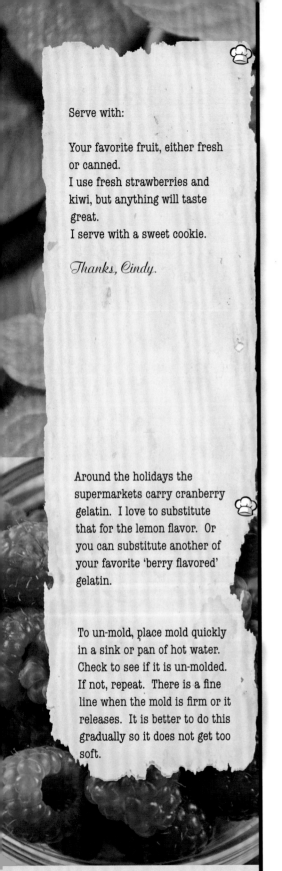

Serve with:

Your favorite fruit, either fresh or canned.
I use fresh strawberries and kiwi, but anything will taste great.
I serve with a sweet cookie.

Thanks, Cindy.

Around the holidays the supermarkets carry cranberry gelatin. I love to substitute that for the lemon flavor. Or you can substitute another of your favorite 'berry flavored' gelatin.

To un-mold, place mold quickly in a sink or pan of hot water. Check to see if it is un-molded. If not, repeat. There is a fine line when the mold is firm or it releases. It is better to do this gradually so it does not get too soft.

Pineapple-Mint Freeze

1 can crushed pineapple (about 2 ½ cups)
2 teaspoons unflavored gelatin
½ cup mint jelly *(see index under jellies)* **or purchase it. green food coloring**
1 cup whipping cream, whipped

Drain pineapple, reserving the juice. In a pot add the juice from pineapple, gelatin, and the mint jelly. Stir with a wire whisk, making sure the gelatin is dissolved. Chill mixture for several hours or until it thickens. Fold in whipped cream and crushed pineapple. Add a few drops of green food coloring. Put into ice cube trays or freeze in a pan overnight. If you have used a pan, cut into 1 inch squares. Serve with other fruits.

©Connie Hope

Cranberry-Raspberry Mold

1   **3 oz package raspberry flavored gelatin**
1   **3 oz package lemon flavored gelatin** *(can use cranberry)*
2   **cups boiling water**
1   **10 oz package fresh or frozen red raspberries**
1   **cup cranberry orange relish** *(see relishes in the index or purchase from your market)*
1   **8 oz bottle of lemon lime carbonated soda** *(about 1 cup)*

Dissolve the raspberry and lemon gelatin in boiling water. Stir in the red raspberries. Separate the frozen berries using a fork. Add the cranberry orange relish. Refrigerate until cold, but not completely set. In a slow, steady motion add the soda and gently stir. Chill again until partially set. Put into a pretty mold and chill overnight. Put lettuce on a decorative plate and un-mold. I have several holiday molds that I use.

Cranberry Mold and variations

2 3 oz packages raspberry gelatin *(or if you can find cranberry gelatin, that is best)*

1 16 oz can whole cranberries

1 16 oz can pineapple, either crushed or chunked

1 can mandarin oranges

2 cups hot water

1 cup reserved liquid plus water to make one cup

Mix gelatin with hot water and stir. Drain oranges, pineapple, and reserve liquid. Add remaining liquid—cold water and cold juices reserve. Refrigerate until starting to gel. Add fruit and fold in gently. *(This way the fruit will not fall to the bottom)* Break up whole cranberries with a fork if needed. Put in mold and chill for at least 4 hours.

There are many variations to this recipe

Add ½ cup of your favorite nuts, broken, but not chopped.

Add ½ cup chopped celery.

Or
Decrease the liquid by about ¼ cup and add ½ cup of frozen whipped topping. This will change the look of the mold. The other mold is transparent. With the addition of the whipped topping, it becomes opaque and pink. It is a little sweeter than the others.

Or
Add 1 cup seedless white or green grapes, cut in half. You can eliminate the oranges and use the grapes or eliminate the pineapple and use the grapes.

Or
Add 1 can of raspberries, fresh or frozen. Eliminate one of the other fruits.

You don't want it too dense with fruit.

You can substitute cranberry juice, the drained juice from the oranges or pineapple, or a little of everything.

All these variation are good and different. Maybe you can think of others.

I use it on my Thanksgiving and Christmas table.

©Connie Hope

Great with a berry sauce on them. *(see desserts under cheese cake)*

Thanks, Maryanne,
for your great pancake recipe and all the times you made this at the mountain house.

Add 1 cup of any vegetable that you like to this recipe.

Suggestions:

Broccoli
Spinach
Asparagus
Or any leftover vegetable

Vegan Quiche
Substitute vegan bacon and vegan cheeses.
1 lb firm tofu for the eggs and soy milk for the cream. Put in blender.

©Connie Hope

Cottage Cheese Pancakes

1 cup cottage cheese

4 eggs

½ cup flour

6 Tablespoons butter

Whisk eggs. Add cottage cheese, flour, and butter. Mix well. Pour a small amount on skillet or pan and heat until done. Makes about 5-6 pancakes depending on size.

Yummy Pancakes

1 egg

2 cups flour (multigrain is best)

2 cups milk

1 Tablespoon molasses

2 Tablespoons sugar

Pinch salt

4 teaspoons baking powder

Whisk egg. Add the remaining ingredients and mix well. Pour a small amount on skillet or pan, heat until done. Make about 8-10 pancakes.

Quiche

Pie shell (buy or make your own)

6 strips bacon, crumbled

4 small white or yellow onion, sliced

4 eggs, separated and lightly beaten

1 ½ cup light cream

3-4 slices boiled ham, chopped

2 cups Swiss cheese, grated *(can use 1 cup each of your favorite cheese)*

Salt and pepper to taste

½ teaspoon basil

½ teaspoon chives

Chill pie crust. Broil 6 strips of bacon, drain and crumble. (Or microwave) Sauté onions. Sprinkle both on the bottom of the pie shell. Combine yolks, cream, ham, cheese, salt, pepper, basil, and chives, fold in whites and pour over bacon and onions. Cook 425 degrees for 15 minutes and 375 for 25 minutes. Makes 6-8 slices

Eleanor's Baked Almonds

Pour boiling water over 1-2 pounds of almonds.
Let soak for awhile.
Spread on cookie sheet to dry overnight.
Put nuts in bowl and coat with small amount of oil.
Spread nuts in layers on cookie sheet.
Preheat oven 400 degrees.
Cook nuts for 7-8 minutes.
Then turn and cook another 7-8 minutes.
Pour cooked nuts into brown paper bag.
Sprinkle heavily with salt.
Toss around and let cool.

Cinnamon Sugar Roasted Pecans

1 egg white

1 teaspoon vanilla

1 teaspoon cold water

1 pound pecans

½ cup sugar

½ teaspoon cinnamon

Pinch salt

Whisk egg white, vanilla, and water until frothy. Stir pecans into wet mixture until coated. Mix sugar, cinnamon, and salt together. Add to pecans and stir until coated. Bake 350 degrees on ungreased cookie sheet for 10-15 minutes. Turn pecans and bake another 10-15 minutes.

Granola

4 cups old-fashioned oats

½ cup sliced almonds (or your favorite nuts)

½ cup packed brown sugar

½ teaspoon salt

½ teaspoon cinnamon

¼ cup oil

¼ cup honey

1 teaspoon vanilla

1 ½ cup raisins

Preheat oven 300 degrees. Mix first five items. In saucepan warm oil and honey. Stir in vanilla. Pour over mix and bake on cookie sheet for 40 minutes, turn every 10 minutes. Cool and stir in raisins.*

I used to work with Eleanor and she made these all the time. They are delicious.

These two recipes are great for gift giving at the holidays. Put them in a fancy jar and decorate with ribbons.

This recipe was given to my friend, Sue. She gave the pecans to me as a holiday gift. I loved them so much and asked for the recipe so I could share with everyone.

This makes a great gift. Fill a jar and add a holiday bow.

Coating may look white on the cinnamon sugar pecans.

Thanks Lois
for your great recipe.

*Substitute anything to equal 1½ cup raisins.
Pecans
Chocolate nuggets'
White nuggets
Cereal

Dried cranberries, cherries, oranges, blueberries, or any other dried fruits.

I remember when I was a kid and my mother used to make this. I always thought it was great. But as we grow older we sometimes forget the little things. A friend, Pat, makes this mix and I remember all things that were associated with it. It is a great ol' time recipe brought back.

P.S. I didn't have microwave directions when I first made this mix.

There are now lots of variations on the original recipe. I am sure that with some imagination, you can think up even more.

Enjoy!

If I have just a little cereal or snack mix left on the shelf, I add that to the mix too.

Original Trail Mix

©Connie Hope

Original Trail Mix

3 cups rice squares cereal
3 cups corn squares cereal
3 cups wheat squares cereal
6 Tablespoons butter or margarine
2-3 Tablespoons Worcestershire sauce
2 teaspoons seasoned salt
1 teaspoon garlic powder
1 teaspoon onion powder
1 cup mixed nuts
1 cup pretzels

There are two sets of directions. Choose the one that suits you. Makes about 3 + quarts of mix.

Oven Directions:
Heat oven to 250 degrees. In a large un-greased roasting pan, melt butter in oven. Stir in seasonings. Gradually stir in remaining ingredients until evenly coated. Bake for 1 hour, stirring every 15 minutes. Spread on paper towels to cool. Store in airtight container.

Microwave Directions:
In a large microwave bowl, heat butter until melted. Stir in seasonings. Gradually stir in remaining ingredients until evenly coated. Microwave for 5-6 minutes stirring every 1-2 minutes. Spread on paper towels to cool. Store in airtight container.

Variations: Use any or some or all of these:

1 cup garlic flavored bite-size bagel chips
1 cup sourdough pretzels, broken in bite-size pieces
1 cup cheese crackers
1 cup mustard-flavor pretzels
1 package ranch dressing and seasoning mix
1-2 cup cheese fish or other flavors
1-2 cup rice crackers with nut mix—this is great
1-2 cups wasabi peas
1 cup almonds
1 cup pecans
1-2 cup whole grain oat cereal 'o's'

More Variations to the Trail Mix:

Spicy Trail Mix:

Add 3 teaspoons red pepper powder mix 2 Tablespoons yellow mustard or spicy mustard. *(your choice)*

Cheese Trail Mix:

2 cups cheese crackers, bite-size
½ cup grated parmesan cheese *(or your choice of cheeses)*

Chili Trail Mix:

¼ cup dry-roasted peanuts
1/3 cup grated parmesan cheese
2-3 teaspoon chili powder
2 more teaspoons garlic powder from original recipe

Chili Trail Mix variation:

Instead of the chili powder use about 3-4 teaspoons of a chili mix. If you like it stronger, experiment.

Taco Trail Mix:

2 cups cheese crackers, bite-size (your choice)
1 cup salted peanuts, dry-roasted if you prefer
1 package taco seasoning mix.

©Connie Hope

This is great to carry in the car for the kids or to have at home watching football.

Your choices are endless. So, have fun with this and experiment.

Ask your kids what they like best in the mix.

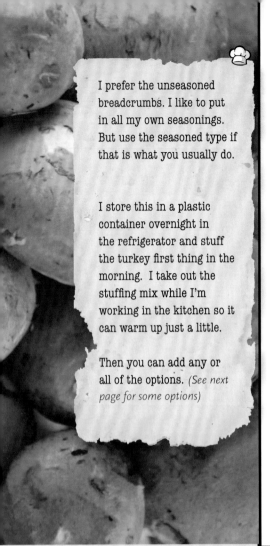

I prefer the unseasoned breadcrumbs. I like to put in all my own seasonings. But use the seasoned type if that is what you usually do.

I store this in a plastic container overnight in the refrigerator and stuff the turkey first thing in the morning. I take out the stuffing mix while I'm working in the kitchen so it can warm up just a little.

Then you can add any or all of the options. *(See next page for some options)*

Connie's Basic Stuffing

1 ½ cups of chopped celery (you can always use more if you like lots)
1 ½ cup chopped white onions
1 cup of chopped mushrooms

Fry all above ingredients in a pan with margarine. Cook until the onion and celery are soft. Set aside in a large bowl.

In another bowl, mix **12 oz bag of cubed bread** (It will stuff a 14 lb turkey.)
1 ½ Tablespoons turkey seasoning (It has a picture of a turkey on the front of the package.)
Pinch of sage
Pinch fresh thyme
Lots of fresh parsley –I cut it with scissors, but you can put it in a chopping blender. (I use half the bunch purchased at the supermarket.)

Mix dry ingredients.
Add **1 stick of melted margarine**
1-2 cups of chicken broth (I just add this until the bread gets moist, but not soaked.)
Salt and pepper to taste.
Mix all ingredients together.
Then stuff the turkey or put stuffing in a casserole dish for baking.

Connie's Basic Stuffing

Options:

Use one, two, or three, or use all of the options listed below. I use the first two for stuffing the turkey. I make a separate casserole of the stuffing with the oyster. It is just that some people don't like oysters. Or you can not tell them that the oysters are in there. Bake covered in the oven at 350 degrees for almost one hour. Then bake uncovered for another thirty minutes or until the top is crispy.

1. Three links of mild Italian sausage—cut in small pieces and fried. This can be done the day ahead and stored in the refrigerator. Sometimes you have to buy five sausages, so I cook them all and freeze two so I can have them on spaghetti sauce.

2. Chestnuts—I go to Williams-Sonoma, get their jar of chestnuts and add them to the stuffing. One jar is good for about a 14 pound turkey. Use two if the turkey is more than that.

3. Oysters—get fresh small oysters in the 8 oz container. Rinse for awhile and drain. Add them to the Basic Stuffing Recipe. Either cook in the turkey or in a casserole with stuffing mix in it. I always have lots of leftover stuffing—I cook an 18-20 lb turkey and I use 1 ½ times the recipe.

No measurements in this recipe are exact. If you like more parsley, add it or if you like more mushrooms, add them, or it you don't like mushrooms, don't use them.

I used to bake the chestnuts for the stuffing. It is a lot of work. You have to puncture each one and place it on a cookie sheet and bake for twenty minutes. Then you have to kill your fingers to pull the shell off. Not worth all that work! Now I go to Williams-Sonoma for 'the jar.'

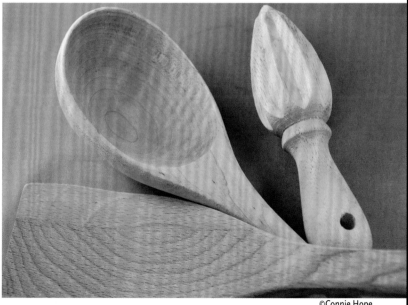

©Connie Hope

Use medium grade vodka for your infusing. Use something that you would drink straight up.

Use only fresh fruit or herbs, not canned items.

You can also make this using a 750 ml bottle of vodka (which is equal to about 8 cups of liquid) and 2-2 ½ cups filled over the top of your fruit or herbs or vegetables

If you crush the berries, it will cloud the liquid.

Also, you can use a few sprigs of rosemary or basil to give a hint of flavor.

Experimentation is the key.
Have fun.

Sugar Syrup
2 cups water
2 cups sugar
Heat until sugar is dissolved.
Boil to 3-4 minutes.
Stir continually.

Cinnamon and apples are another interesting combination.

The pepper vodka makes a great Bloody Mary.

They make glass containers with a spout that can be used for serving.

Infusing Vodka with your own flavors

Customize the vodka and make your own tastes. It's easy. All you need is your favorite brand of vodka, a glass container, some fruit and a willing palate. You can share and tell what you have added to your favorite vodka to all your friends. Or you can keep them guessing if you'd like.

½ cup fruit or herbs or vegetables
2 cups vodka

Clean and chop the fruit, herbs, or vegetables Wash a glass jar well and add the fruit, herbs, or vegetables. Pour the vodka over the top and screw lid tightly. Refrigerate for 4-5 days. Can be kept for up to four weeks in the refrigerator before it starts to turn bitter. Taste frequently to check if the infusion is completed.

Some suggestions:
You can use cantaloupes, peaches, cherries, strawberries, blueberries, raspberries pineapples, mango, vanilla beans, or blackberries. Also try lemon, lime, grapefruit, fresh ginger, lemon-grass, or chili peppers. Use your imagination. If you don't like it, try something else. Have fun!

Lavender Vodka

750 ml vodka
¾-1 cup sugar syrup (see on left side)
3 Tablespoons of lavender buds, dried or fresh.

Pepper Vodka

1 Serrano chili, seeded, stemmed, and cut in quarters
1 jalapeno chili, seeded, stemmed, and cut in quarters
1 red habanero chili, seeded, stemmed and cut in quarters
1 bottle vodka

Put cut chilies in a glass container. Pour bottle of vodka over the peppers. Cap tightly. Let stand at room temperature for 36-48 hours Make sure to shake gently one to two times a day. Do not allow it to infuse over one week as it will taste bitter. Strain, put into original bottle, cap tightly, and refrigerate.

Worcestershire Butter *(vegetable topping)*

¼ cup butter, melted

½ teaspoon minced garlic *(either fresh or the canned type)*

2 ½ teaspoons of Worcestershire sauce *(use your favorite)*

¼ cup of bread crumbs *(either purchased or old bread)*

Melt butter. Add Worcestershire sauce and garlic. Simmer in a pot for a few minutes. Steam vegetables of your choice. Add to vegetables about 3 Table-spoons of butter, toss to melt. Add bread crumbs to Worcestershire sauce. Sprinkle over steamed vegetables.

Zucchini Spread

1 cup finely grated zucchini *(clean outside)*

1 cup shredded cheddar cheese

½ cup chopped walnuts *(You can also use pecans)*

1 teaspoon lemon juice

¾ cup mayonnaise

Salt and pepper to taste

Grate zucchini and put on a paper towel to remove as much moisture as possible. Combine all ingredients and mix well. Cover and put in refrigerator for 1- ½ hours. Dip raw veggies or use crackers.

Serve with:
Cauliflower
Broccoli
Steamed peppers
Celery
Brussels Sprouts
Green Beans
Any vegetable your family enjoys.

Serve with:

Topping on a baked potato
Ham or pork chops
Melba toast and crackers
Dip vegetables

Zucchini Spread

©Connie Hope

©Connie Hope

©Connie Hope

Connie's Cooking Tips:

■ To make pancakes fluffier and lighter, substitute club soda for half of the milk in the recipe.

■ Most ovens are not true with their temperature. It is a good idea to check the temperature of your oven so when you cook something that is temperature sensitive such as cookies or cake you can compensate for the difference. To check the temperature in your oven, purchase an oven thermometer from a kitchen store in your area. It is a $4.00 or $5.00 purchase that is well worth your while.

■ Equivalents: Rule of thumb for measurements

1. One pound of flour is equivalent to about four cups.

2. Each one cup of dry beans or peas you put into a recipe,
   it will make   about two and one half cups cooked.

3. One cup of uncooked white rice makes about three cups cooked.

4. One pound of sugar is equivalent to about two cups.

5. Eight ounces of uncooked pasta makes about three and a half to four cups cooked. Your average box of pasta is 16 ounces. If you cook half the box you will have around four cups of pasta. Have you even put the entire box of pasta in a pot and had pasta for two or three nights... I'll never tell.

Appendix

"Chocolate cream pie! You know what I love about cooking? I love that after a day when nothing is sure and when I say nothing, I mean nothing. You can come home and absolutely know that if you add egg yolks to chocolate and sugar and milk, it will get thick. That's such a comfort."

Julie Powell in Julie & Julia

©Connie Hope

Equivalents

Dash = less than 1/8 teaspoon
3 teaspoons = 1 Tablespoon
16 Tablespoons = 1 cup
1 cup = ½ pint
2 cups = 1 pint
2 pints (4 cups)= 1 quart
4 quarts = 1 gallon
8 quarts = 1 peck
4 pecks = bushel
16 oz = 1 pound

4 Tablespoons = ¼ cup
5 1/3 Tablespoons = 1/3 cup
8 teaspoons= ½ cup
10 2/3 Tablespoons =2/3 cup
12 Tablespoons = ¾ cup
14 Tablespoons= 7/8 cup
16 Tablespoons = 1 cup

Apples 1 pound = 3 medium apples or about 2-3 cups depending on how they are sliced

Lemon, medium
Juice of one = 2-3 Tablespoons of lemon
Rind, lightly grated 1½-3 teaspoons

Sugar 1 pound = 2 cups
Brown sugar   1 lb = 2 ¼ cups firmly packed

Dates 1 pound = 2 ¼ cups
Prunes 1 pound = 2 1/3 cups
Raisins 15 oz package = 3 cups
Candied peels ½ lb = 1 ½ cups
Candied fruit ½ lb = 1 ½ cups

Contents of Cans
Most common are:
8 oz = 1 cup
12 oz = 1 ½ cups
14-16 oz = 1 ¾ cups
16-17 oz = 2 cups
1 lb 4 oz = 2 ½ cups

©Connie Hope

Home Canning

Years ago, people stated they were 'putting something by' when they were canning fruits and vegetables. There are many methods of 'putting something by.' Two are safer methods—the Steam Pressure Cooking Method and the Water Bath Method. I will go into detail and give you a quick lesson on home canning. It is a great method to keep jellies and jam over an extended amount of time.

Home canning is a great method to preserve fresh fruits and vegetables, whether they have come from your garden, from neighbors who have extra fruit on their trees, or if all else fails you have stopped at your favorite food market. Always choose only fresh and perfect fruits and vegetables for canning. Wash them thoroughly when preparing for the canning process. The jars don't have to be new. In fact, you can often find a bargain at garage sales or flea markets.

The basic principle is to expose the fruits and vegetable to a high temperature that will stop the food from decaying and kill bacteria. The fruits and vegetables are packed into sterile, airtight glass jars with removable seals and ringed bands. I am sure there are many manufacturers of glass jars, but a few that come to mind are Blue Ball and Kerr. Most stores carry these items. Make sure the jars and rings are clean. I simply run them thorough a cycle in my dishwasher. Always make sure that your jar rim is clean after filling it and has no residue of jelly or jam on it before you put on the removable top. This will create a good seal when heated. A jar improperly sealed will allow the food to spoil.

For canning, foods are classified into two groups—acid and low acid.

Acid foods, like fruit, some tomatoes, sauerkraut, and pickled vegetables can be safely processed by boiling. The types of organisms that cause spoilage in these foods are usually killed at boiling temperatures. Use the boiling water bath method for canning acid foods.

I just found ten small canning jars at a garage sale for fifty cents. They run anywhere from $6.00 to $8.00 for twelve jars in the store. What a steal!

©Connie Hope

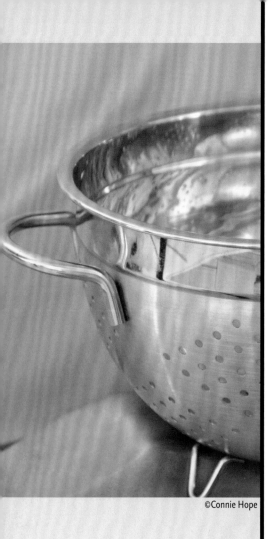

©Connie Hope

Some tomatoes are on the borderline between being acid and a low acid. These products need added acid so that they can be safely processed in a water bath canner. The addition of low-acid vegetables such as peppers, onions, and celery may lower the acid level to the point that processing the food in a pressure canner may be necessary. Current recommendations for acidification of whole, crushed, or juiced tomatoes are to add 2 Tablespoons of bottled lemon juice or ½ teaspoon citric acid per quart of tomatoes. For pints use 1 Tablespoon bottled lemon juice or ¼ teaspoon citric acid. Low acid foods such as vegetable and some low acid tomatoes must be processed in a pressure canner. If vinegar and small amounts of these vegetables are added in a recipe, processing in a boiling water bath may be safe. If the vinegar changes the taste of the food, then small amounts of sugar can be added.

I usually do not process the chutneys and salsas for this reason. I don't take chances.

Low acid foods are most vegetables, meat, and poultry. They require temperatures of 240 degrees F reached at 10 pounds of pressure to be safely processed. They should be pressure cooked.

The sterilized glass jars are exposed to heat by two methods.
Let's look a little closer at each method-- pressure cooker and water bath process. Sometimes with jellies or jams you can put wax-paraffin on the top of them. I don't prefer this method as things can spoil and mold very easily and do not keep as long.

The pressure cooker canning method is used for low acid food which is most vegetables such as beans, beets, corn, all meats and other low acid food. This method processes food under pressure at a temperature around 240 degrees F and more. The cooker supplies enough heat to destroy the bacteria which can cause botulism and other spoilages. I would always use a pressure cooker for low acidic foods. Keep in mind the equipment is much more expensive.

For the recipes in my book, I have used the water bath method. The water bath method processes food at a temperature around 212 degrees F. This method is recommended by Kerr and Blue Ball for fruits, some tomatoes, pickles and relishes and other acidic foods. If there are questions about acidity, don't water bath. I simply refrigerate and use the item in one to three weeks. I usually use half pint jars for gifts and pint jars for my own use.

Method for Water Bathing

1. Use a canning rack to keep jars from touching the bottom of pot.

2. Put the jars with rings and seals into canner with the simmering water. Make sure the water is about one inch above the highest jar.

3. Bring water to a full boil. Set timer and process for recommended time according to the recipe. Most recipes are between 15-30 minutes, but a little over is acceptable.

4. When the time is up, carefully remove jars.

5. Put a towel under and over the jars so they cool gradually. As the jars cool, the contents contract, a vacuum is created, and the seal is locked.

6. After jars are cooled, remove screw band, wipe jars, clean, label and date.

7. Store jars in a cool dry area and use within six months to a year. Rings can be reused, but never reuse the lids.

There are several methods for checking the seal on the jar to make sure it is tight.

■ Hear the seal—The lid snaps down or 'plinks' while the jar is cooling. You can tap the lid with a spoon when the jar has cooled. The clear ringing sound means a seal.

■ Observe the seal—The lid should be curved downward, which means it has sealed.

■ Feel the seal—After the jar has cooled, press the center of the lid. If the lid is down and will not move, the jar is sealed.

The canning equipment can be purchased at most kitchen stores. If you are going to do this for the long haul, I suggest investing in the 'large blue kettle' with lid and with its own rack, a wide-mouth funnel and a pair of tongs. The rack is used to hold the jar off the bottom of the pot and to allow the water to circulate freely. You can also buy just a rack that will fit in any of your current pots.

©Connie Hope

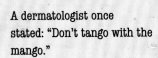
"How to Cut a Mango"

The mango is in the same plant family as poison ivy and its peel can indeed cause allergic skin rashes similar to poison ivy. That's especially true for people who are particularly sensitive to urushiol, the chemical involved. For this reason, it's best to peel a mango before eating it! Perhaps use gloves to cut the skin off and cut into the mango.

Mangos have one long, flat seed which is in the center of the fruit. Cut around the seed to get to the fleshy part or cheek. Then cut around the seed on the opposite side of the mango.

Always use a clean knife.

1. **Stand the mango stem end down on a cutting board. Place knife about ¼ inch from a imaginary center line and cut down through the mango.**

2. **Flip the mango around and cut the other side about ¼ inch from the center. These two sides are sometimes called the cheeks of the mango.**

©Connie Hope

How to Cut a Mango" continued

3. Cut parallel slices with a sharp knife into the mango flesh.
   First cut top to bottom, then across. You will now have many squares.
   Please be careful not to cut through the skin.

4. Scoop the mango squares from the skin with a large spoon.

5. Next, cut around the large seed so you use all pieces of the mango.

©Connie Hope

Jane's Krazy Mixed-Up Seasonings®
Sweet Lime Pepper

Distributed by Flavor Delite, Inc. 578B L & C Distribution Park, Richburg, S.C. 29729 1-800-257-6174 ext 225. Can be purchased in some supermarkets or specialty stores.

©Connie Hope

Picture below is a fruit squeezer used on lemons and limes to remove all the juice and pulp. It works well! It's the one tool I would never live without.

©Connie Hope

Spoon Drip Test for Jelly Point (Gel Point) or Sheet Test

Pictures by John Hope

1. Take a spoon of jelly liquid and let most of it return to the pot leaving a small amount on the spoon. Move the spoon around in a swirling motion. This allows the liquid to cool.

2. The liquid will start to cool and become heavier and show signs of starting to 'sheet' on the spoon. Sheeting means it starts to look like it is going to stay in a droplet on the spoon, but it does not quite stay on the spoon.

3. When the jelly point (Gel Point) is reached, the jelly will stay on the spoon and the droplets of two or more come together.

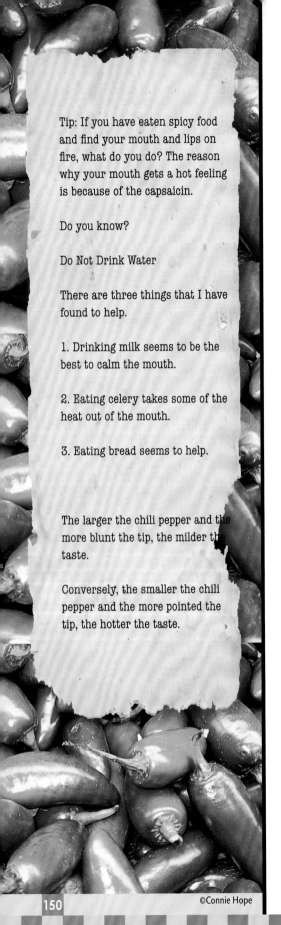

Tip: If you have eaten spicy food and find your mouth and lips on fire, what do you do? The reason why your mouth gets a hot feeling is because of the capsaicin.

Do you know?

Do Not Drink Water

There are three things that I have found to help.

1. Drinking milk seems to be the best to calm the mouth.

2. Eating celery takes some of the heat out of the mouth.

3. Eating bread seems to help.

The larger the chili pepper and the more blunt the tip, the milder the taste.

Conversely, the smaller the chili pepper and the more pointed the tip, the hotter the taste.

What Makes a Pepper Hot?

The Scoville Scale is a measurement of the hotness or pungency of chili peppers. This scale was named after its creator, American pharmacist Wilbur Scoville. He developed this scale in 1912 while working at Park Davis, now Pfizer.

It measures the 'capsaicin,' which stimulates nerve endings in the skin and gives chili peppers their heat. The number of Scoville heat units on the scale indicates the amount of 'capsaicin' present in the pepper. Hence the heat that the peppers have. It is based on the amount of dilution it would take for the pepper to be unnoticed by the panel of tasters.

I have listed a chart below of some of the peppers listed in my recipes to show their heat scale. The bell pepper rates 'O' on the chart and the Habanera rates 100,000 to 300,000.

Scale	Name
5,300,000	Police Grade Pepper Spray
2,000,000	Common Pepper Spray
100,000-300,000	Habanera
100,000-350,000	Scotch Bonnet
30,000-50,000	Cayenne, Tabasco
15,000-30,000	Crushed red pepper
5,000-15,000	Serrano, Yellow Hat Wax
2,500-10,000	Jalapeno Peppers
500-1,000	New Mexico Peppers
100-500	Cherry peppers
O	Bell Peppers, Pimentos

- Research done on the Internet.
- Wikipedia

Cutting and Baking Pumpkin

Here is how to cut and use fresh pumpkin for soups and other dishes. Use a sharp knife and cut the top at an angle to form the lid. I always cut looking down at the pumpkin. That way the angle is easy to achieve. Let the stem be the handle.

Remove the 'gut' and fibers and seeds of the pumpkin.
(I save the seeds to bake them-see next page)
If you are using the pumpkin as a soup tureen, it is easiest to use a melon baller and scrape the inside of the pumpkin to about ½ inch from the skin. If you are only going to use the meat from the pumpkin, you can cut the pumpkin into quarters. Place either the meat from the pumpkin or the pieces on a cookie sheet to bake. There are three methods that you can cook pumpkin and puree to use either in pie, soups or baking.

Three Cooking Methods for Pumpkin:

1. Baking Pumpkin Method
Put the quarters of the pumpkin on a cookie sheet and cover with foil. Bake at 375 degrees for about 1 ½ hours for the quartered pumpkin and 1 hour *(if you have melon balls)* or until tender. Once the pumpkin has cooled, puree it in a food processor. For a smoother consistency for soups or baking you can press the pumpkin through a sieve.

2. Boiling Pumpkin Method
If you have quartered the pumpkin cut into chunks or if you have balled it, it is already in chunks. Place in a pot and cover with water. Bring to a boil and cook until tender. Let chucks cool then puree in food processor.

3. Microwave Pumpkin Method
If you have quartered the pumpkin or balled it, put it in a bowl and microwave for about 6 minutes. Check to see if tender, repeat if needed. Puree in food processor.

Pumpkins are not always in season, so when they are, I really have fun with these recipes.

If you are not using the pureed pumpkin immediately, you can refrigerate it for up to three days or freeze it for several months. In this way you will have that fall pumpkin into the winter months.

©Connie Hope

Connie's Cooking Tips:

■ Choose smaller pumpkins for cooking and eating.

■ Pumpkin seeds known as "pepitas" can be roasted and eaten as snacks. *(see page 83)*

■ Pumpkin pie was served at the Pilgrim's second Thanksgiving in 1623 and is still a Thanksgiving feast tradition.

■ A 5 pound pumpkin yields 4-4 ½ cups of pureed, cooked pumpkin. One can of 15-16 ounces pumpkin yields about 2 cups of pureed pumpkin.

■ An average mango yields about 1 ½ to 1 ¾ cup diced fruit

■ Mango juice will stain clothing. Be careful when you eat this delicious fruit.

■ Mango skin is not eaten. It can be irritating to the mouth.

■ Soften hardened brown sugar by placing a piece of bread in the box and closing it tight. Allow to stay in the box overnight. The bread will soak up most of the moisture from the brown sugar.

■ After canning, check the seal on every jar to make sure they are air tight. When you push down on a self sealing lid, it should stay down.

©Connie Hope

Index

Forbidden fruit creates many jams.

153

Index

Chutney

D

Desserts

Desserts-Things to be used with them
Pound cake, puddings, cheesecake

Dips

E

F

Fish—Things to be used with them

G

H

Ham—Things that go well with it

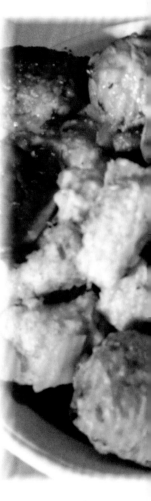

Vegetables and Starch

W

Y

Z

About the Author

Constance L. Hope, known to most as Connie or some even as Con. I was born and raised in a small borough in New Jersey called Metuchen—'The Brainy Borough.' I graduated from Metuchen High School in 1965 and am in the middle of trying to organize our class reunion for 2010. Wow! Time has really flown. And what a great time it has been.

As a child, when my mother would be in the kitchen I was there. I stood on a chair cooking, baking, or sometimes just making a mess. I loved to be by her side and help with any kind of cooking. I learned to create my own special tomato soup from a can of Campbell's® and my imagination. I would add a little of this spice or that sauce to make my own concoction. My father was the tester. Bless his heart..... some of the things, I dare say, were not that good. But as I grew, I learned more about herbs and spices and how to create different taste treats.

I have cooked and catered dinner parties for myself and others. I have been involved with 'Mothers of Twins' cookbook and other cookbooks along my way.

Life has really been great for me. Oh, I have had many ups and downs, but I have my health, my sense of humor and my smile, so it's not all that bad.

After high school, I went to Union Junior College. 'Uicy Juicy' as we called it, located in Cranford, New Jersey. After two years, I transferred to Trenton State College and went to school nights while I worked during the days.

I moved to Doylestown, Pennsylvania, to marry my high school sweetheart. So much for high school sweethearts! I re-married several years later and lived in Huntingdon Valley, Pennsylvania, where I raised three wonderful children. John, my oldest son, has done a lot of the art work for this book. Then I had twins, Jacob and Jennifer. Jacob has always said to me "Mom, you should write a cookbook because you make the best sides and soups ever." So with his suggestion, I have created my book. And Jennifer, who is now a lawyer, has helped me with some of the legal issues about the book.

They all grew up standing on chairs in my kitchen helping me make cookies or soup or homemade jellies and jams. Each with an apron and flour or fruit all over them, as well as the floor.

Through the years, I have traveled a great deal and collected, tried, changed, and created new recipes from friends and acquaintances all over the world. Most recently, Hewitt, partner of 15 years, and proofreader for this book, (Thanks!) and I moved to Ft. Myers, Florida, where the weather is warm, the fruit is abundant, and the time was available for me to write and put together this cookbook. It has been twenty years in the writing, but it has been well worth the long creation time.

Cooking is something that you need to get into to enjoy. I have always loved to cook and tried to instill this love in my children. I am now trying to instill that love in each of you. By reading and creating with some of my favorite recipes, I hope you will make them yours. Good luck on your tasting and cooking journey.

Enjoy!

Connie Hope